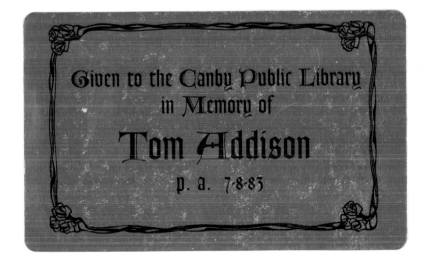

The Children's Dictionary of

Mythology

David Adams Leeming
General Editor

Marilee Foglesong
Former Young Adult Coordinator for the New York Public Library
Advisor

Frankin Watts
A Division of Grolier Publishing
New York   London   Hong Kong   Sydney
Danbury, Connecticut

DEVELOPED, DESIGNED, AND PRODUCED BY
BOOK BUILDERS INCORPORATED

Visit Franklin Watts on the Internet at
http://publishing.grolier.com

Library of Congress Cataloging-in-Publication Data

The children's dictionary of mythology / general editor, David
Adams Leeming.
     p. cm.
    Includes bibliographical references and index.
    Summary: A dictionary of terms, names, and places in the
mythology of various cultures around the world.
    ISBN 0-531-11708-1
    1. Mythology Dictionaries. Juvenile. [1. Mythology
Dictionaries.]   I. Leeming, David Adams, 1937– .
BL 303.C435   1999
291.1'3'03--dc21   99-25034
                                             CIP

Contents

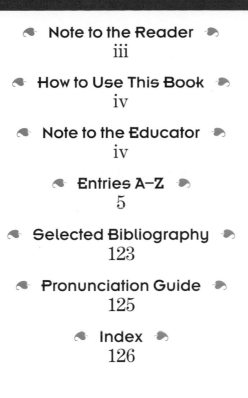
Note to the Reader

Myths are sacred tales about gods, goddesses, heroes, and heroines. People have told myths since ancient times in order to explain where humans and animals came from, how the world was made, and suggest how people should behave.

People in all parts of the world have myths. The collection of myths that belongs to a particular culture is called a mythology. This dictionary will introduce you to various mythological characters, places, and ideas of many different cultures—from the ancient Greeks and Romans to the Chinese to the Native Americans of North and South America.

While using the dictionary, think about your dreams. Dreams are like personal myths—full of beautiful, unbelievable, and sometimes frightening adventures—and you are the hero. As you learn more about mythology, consider how the stories of gods, goddesses, heroes, and heroines might really be stories about you or people you know.

How to Use This Book

The entries in this book are arranged in alphabetical order. They identify characters and places, explain ideas, and retell the stories handed down for generations. Some stories about characters, such as the LABORS OF HERCULES, and important cultural myths, such as EGYPTIAN CREATION MYTHS and INCAN FLOOD, are highlighted. These feature stories appear in colored boxes, either near a character's alphabetical entry or close to the story's alphabetical order.

Many of the names are difficult to pronounce. You do not need to pronounce them correctly right from the start. So if a name looks difficult, you should begin by pronouncing it as it sounds in your head. After the title of most entries, you will find the pronunciation of difficult words. A pronunciation guide at the back of the book will help you use these spellings.

Most entries contain CROSS-REFERENCES. These are words or phrases in small capital letters that point to related subjects discussed elsewhere in the dictionary. Whenever you see a cross-reference, in the text or at the end of an entry, you can find more information on that topic in a separate entry. The index at the back of the book also will help you locate topics.

Note to the Educator

This dictionary is intended as a general introduction to mythology. The entries include descriptions of cultures with which particular mythologies are associated, summaries of major myths, and identifications of important mythological characters, places, objects, and themes. Our purpose has been to touch not only on the mythologies many of us already know, those of Ancient Greece and Rome for example, but also on the great sagas of ancient Egypt and Sumerian, those of India, Japan, and China, and those of Australia, Africa, the Americas, and the South Pacific.

At the basis of our work is an assumption that mythologies are more than odd collections of narratives. The word mythology does not stand opposite religion. The use of one word or the other does not suggest "truth." A mythology reflects a given society's view of itself. The terms of a culture's mythology naturally reflect the world of that culture. Coyotes play a large role in Native American mythologies, the Nile is central to Egyptian mythology, darkness and cold mark the myths of the Norse people. In a sense, myths are societal dreams. They emerge from the subconscious of the collective mind of a culture and reflect the deepest concerns and beliefs of that mind.

David A. Leeming

Achilles (ə kil´ ēz) 🐦 The son of Peleus and Thetis, Achilles was a Greek hero who fought in the Trojan War. When he was a child, his mother dipped him into the Styx, the river of the Underworld. Because of this Achilles could not be harmed—except on the heel by which she held him (it did not touch the water). He died after being wounded in his "Achilles heel" by the Trojan prince Paris. [*See also* GREEK MYTHOLOGY; *ILIAD*; UNDERWORLD, DESCENT TO.]

Adam (ad´ əm) 🐦 In the Hebrew CREATION story found in the Bible, Adam was the first man. Created by God, Adam and the first woman, EVE, were the parents of the human race. They originally lived in the Garden of Eden. However, they ate fruit that God had forbidden to them and were expelled. [*See also* FATHER GOD; *LEAB-HAR GABHALA*; WORLD PARENTS.]

Adonis (ə do´ nəs) 🐦 A beautiful youth in GREEK MYTHOLOGY, Adonis was loved from the time of his birth by APHRODITE, the goddess of love. Mortally wounded by a boar while hunting, PERSEPHONE restored him to life on the condition that he spend half of each year with her and the other half with Aphrodite. [*See also* APHRODITE AND ADONIS.]

Aeneas (i nē´ us) 🐦 A hero in both Greek and Roman mythology, Aeneas was the son of the Trojan mortal Anchises and the goddess APHRODITE. Aeneas showed great courage in defending Troy during the Trojan war. Afterward, he went to Italy and is said to have founded the bloodline of the Roman people. Virgil's epic poem, the *AENEID*, was named for Aeneas. [*See also* AENEAS, QUEST OF.]

Aeneid (i nē´ id) 🐦 An epic poem in Latin by Virgil, the *Aeneid* is an account of a quest for a new CITY to replace the lost Troy. Written in the first century B.C., the *Aeneid* is a Roman counterpart of the Greek epics the *ILIAD* and the *ODYSSEY*. It relates the adventures of AENEAS after the Trojan War. Although Virgil died before completing it, the Romans regarded the *Aeneid* as their most important literary work. [*See also* AENEAS, QUEST OF.]

African Mythology 🐦 Developed by many different tribal cultures, the myths of Africa often

Acoma Creation Myth (a′ kōm ä)

According to the CREATION story of the Acoma Indians of North America, the ancestors of the human race first lived in worlds within the earth. Eventually, the ancestors emerged, pushing their way to the surface. As in other such EMERGENCE myths, the earth was the mother, the source of the creative power.

Latiku, the Great Mother of the human race, showed them how to keep records of their families through the maternal line. She gave each clan an animal or plant name. The male head of the Antelope clan became the father of powerful spirits called KACHINAS. [*See also* GREAT GODDESS; NATIVE NORTH AMERICAN MYTHOLOGY.]

share stories or characters. Many of these myths describe CREATION and the SEPARATION OF HEAVEN AND EARTH. They express a strong belief in an AFTERLIFE and give reasons for such things as death and disease. Other stories explain why certain animals look or act as they do.

An African myth might have a human HERO AND HEROINE, or might include humans, animals, and deities, all of whom behave much alike. TRICK-STERS are especially popular characters in many African myths. [*See also* AMMA; ANANSE; DOGON CREATION MYTH; LEGBA; LITUOLONE; MWINDO; WANJIRU; WULBARI.]

Afterlife 🐾 Most cultures throughout the world have some concept of an afterlife—an existence after death. People as distant from one another as the Greeks and the Maya have described an "underworld" where

This painting from an ancient Egyptian tomb shows servants carrying food to the dead.

Quest of Aeneas (i nē´ us)

According to Roman mythology, AENEAS was the only Trojan chieftain to escape the fall of Troy. While the victorious Greeks destroyed the city, Aeneas fled with his son and his father, Anchises.

Aeneas and a band of Trojan refugees set sail on a QUEST to Italy to found a new city. The voyage there was dangerous and difficult. Aeneas' father Anchises died along the way. In Sicily, Aeneas and his followers were almost eaten by one of the CYCLOPES.

A storm at sea blew Aeneas' ships off course, causing them to land on the coast of Africa. There Aeneas met DIDO, the queen of Carthage. Dido fell in love with Aeneas, who basked in her attentions for a time. When he abandoned her to continue on his quest, she killed herself.

Soon after his arrival in Italy, Aeneas made a trip to the Underworld. Guided by the SIBYL of Cumae, Aeneas survived the trip and met his father. Anchises gave Aeneas valuable advice and showed him the spirits of his descendants.

Aeneas then went to the city of Latium and befriended King Latinus. Latinus recognized Aeneas as a man of destiny and offered him his daughter, Lavinia, in marriage. But the marriage was opposed by her suitor, Turnus.

Turnus made war on Aeneas and the Trojans. Eventually, Aeneas slew Turnus in single combat, bringing victory to the Trojans. The Romans believed that Aeneas married Lavinia after his victory. Together, they founded the race of Romans. [*See also* DREAMING; JOURNEY QUEST; UNDERWORLD, DESCENT TO.]

people go when they die. The afterlife might be in a mythic place such as Valhalla in NORSE MYTHOLOGY or the Elysian Fields in GREEK MYTHOLOGY. Afterlife myths vary tremendously from culture to culture, but they often feature rewards or punishments for behavior during life. In ancient Egypt mummies were buried with the *BOOK OF THE DEAD*, a guide to the afterlife. [*See also* AFRICAN MYTHOLOGY; EGYPTIAN MYTHOLOGY; HADES; UNDERWORLD, DESCENT TO.]

Alcestis (al ses´ təs)

The wife of Admetus, the king of Pherae in Thessaly, Alcestis agreed to die for her husband. This was because Admetus had learned that he would be immortal if somebody would die in his place. Not knowing the reason for Alcestis' death, HERCULES went to the Underworld and rescued her. She became the subject of a Greek tragedy, *Alcestis*, written by Euripides. [*See also* GREEK MYTHOLOGY; REBIRTH AND RESURRECTION; UNDERWORLD, DESCENT TO.]

Amaterasu (ə mä tėr ä´ sü)

The beautiful Sun Goddess in JAPANESE MYTHOLOGY, Amaterasu was the daughter of IZANAMI AND IZANAGI. Amaterasu walked up a rainbow bridge to the heavens, where she ruled over the other gods and the universe. [*See also* JAPANESE CREATION MYTHS; *NIHONGI*.]

Amma (ä´ mə)

In the mythology of the Dogon and Mande of Africa, Amma was a FATHER GOD who used

Tales of Ananse (ä nän´ sā)

The spider ANANSE of AFRICAN MYTHOLOGY was the subject of many stories. In one tale, Ananse was responsible for people even having stories to tell. One day he decided to buy a box of stories from the Sky God. The price included a python, a leopard, a fairy, and a hornet. Ananse boasted that he would not only capture these creatures and pay the price, he would include his own mother in the trade as well.

With the help of his wife, Aso, Ananse captured each creature and paid the Sky God. He caught the fairy with a doll covered with sticky resin from a tree. When the fairy slapped the doll because it would not speak, she stuck fast.

Ananse sent his mother into heaven and then took the box of stories to his people. From that time on, they were called spider stories. When Ananse opened the box, the stories flew out and scattered. Ananse's people caught some of them, including this one—the story of the stories.

In another myth Ananse started with a single ear of corn. Using deception, he traded one thing for another until he had 1,000 slaves. He gave the slaves to the god WULBARI but boasted that he was even smarter than the god. Annoyed, Wulbari demanded that Ananse bring him "something" without saying what that something was. Ananse disguised himself as a bird, sneaked close to Wulbari, and overheard the god say he wanted the Sun, Moon, and darkness. Everyone was impressed when Ananse returned and drew these gifts out of his bag. Several people, however, were blinded by the nearness of the sun; that is how blindness first came into our world.

Many other stories are told about Ananse. Sometimes he wins, but his boastfulness often gets him into trouble.

both sacred words and handcrafts to create the universe. Amma invented pottery in order to make the sun and moon. [See also AFRICAN MYTHOLOGY; DOGON CREATION MYTH.]

Ananse (ä nän´ sā) ☙ In AFRICAN MYTHOLOGY, Ananse the spider was an important TRICKSTER character. Ananse's stories have spread from the Ashanti of Ghana to other parts of Africa, as well as to the Americas. In some areas Ananse was simply known as Spider. [See also ANANSE, TALES OF.]

Ancestor Worship ☙ The practice of honoring or worshiping ancestors is found in cultures around the world. Many people have believed that their dead ancestors existed in an AFTERLIFE and could influence the world of the living. SHAMANS were thought to be able to contact the spirits of these dead ancestors. Religious beliefs and the accompanying rituals connected to ancestor worship are called ancestor cults.

The ancient Romans called their ancestor worship manism. In ancient China, only ancestors of the royal families were worshiped at first. But by the third century B.C., ancestors of all Chinese classes were included. Chinese ancestor worship still continues in Hong Kong.

Ancestors are worshiped today by other cultures all over the world, in places such as India, Japan, Sri Lanka, Southeast Asia, the islands of the Pacific, and Africa.

Animism (an´ ə miz əm) 🗣 The belief that everything in nature has a soul or spirit is called animism. Early peoples believed that these spirits could be contacted through human SHAMANS, or wise ones. The spirits gradually took on personalities such as "old man of rocks" or "cloud woman." [*See also* JAPANESE MYTHOLOGY.]

Aphrodite (af rə dīt´ ē) 🗣 The Greek goddess of love, Aphrodite was known for her great beauty. The daughter of ZEUS, her sons were Eros

According to some myths, the goddess Aphrodite rose fully grown from the sea.

Apache Creation Myths (ə pach´ ē)

The CREATION myths of the Apache Indians of North America varied from one area to another. The four major groupings of Apache culture were the Jicarilla, Chiricahua, Mescalero, and Lipon.

Many Apache creation stories began with supernatural beings called Hactcin, similar to kachinas of the Hopi Indians, who first lived in the CHAOS of PRIMAL WATERS. In myths told by the Jicarilla, the Hactcin created the world, the earth, the Underworld, and the sky. The most powerful of them, Black Hactcin, made the animals and birds out of clay and taught them to walk and fly. When those creatures wanted companionship, Black Hactcin created people. All of this took place in the dark beneath the earth. Then White Hactcin led the people and animals to the surface. A Hactcin myth told by the Chiricahua also included a story about a great flood.

In another EMERGENCE story told by the Jicarilla, the animals and people living underground discovered a hole that led to the surface of the earth. With the help of a buffalo, they finally climbed up and broke though.

In Mescalero Apache stories, Great Spirit created Father Sun, Mother Earth, thunder and lightning, animals, and people—all in four days. The White Mountain Apaches thought of the universe as a sacred lodge. Their creation story featured Four Grandfathers, who represented the four seasons and the four directions. In a Lipon Apache myth, the Four Grandfathers led the emergence from the Underworld to the earth's surface. [*See also* ACOMA CREATION MYTH; CHEROKEE CREATION MYTHS; CORN MOTHER; HOPI EMERGENCE; KIOWA CREATION MYTHS; NATIVE NORTH AMERICAN MYTHOLOGY; NAVAJO EMERGENCE; SIOUX CREATION MYTHS; ZUNI CREATION MYTHS.]

Aphrodite and Adonis
(af rə dīt´ ē) (ə do´ nəs)

According to GREEK MYTHOLOGY, the goddess APHRODITE fell in love with a mortal named ADONIS. This happened when she was accidentally wounded by an arrow shot from the bow of her son, Cupid.

Aphrodite entrusted Adonis to the care of PERSEPHONE, the goddess of the Underworld. Unfortunately, Persephone also fell in love with Adonis and refused to give him back. The god ZEUS stepped in to settle the quarrel. He decided that Adonis would spend every fall and winter in the Underworld with Persephone and every spring and summer among the living with Aphrodite. And so things went for a number of years.

During the spring and summer, Adonis loved to hunt, and Aphrodite usually watched over his safety. But one day, Adonis pursued a fierce boar while Aphrodite was not watching. He only wounded the boar with his spear, and the beast impaled him with its tusks. Aphrodite heard Adonis' death groans and hurried to his side, but it was too late. The youth died in her arms. Where his blood stained the ground, beautiful red flowers grew at Aphrodite's command. These flowers are known as anemones. [*See also* CUPID AND PSYCHE; HYACINTHUS; NARCISSUS; REBIRTH AND RESURRECTION; ROMAN AND ETRUSCAN MYTHOLOGY.]

(or Cupid) and AENEAS. In Roman mythology, Aphrodite is known as Venus. [*See also* APHRODITE AND ADONIS; GREEK MYTHOLOGY; HEPHAESTUS.]

Apocalypse   (a päk´ ə lips)

The violent destruction of the world, or a prophecy of that ending, is called the Apocalypse. In most stories about the Apocalypse, a deity ended (or will end) the world to punish evil or correct errors in CREATION. The Apocalypse was generally seen as a cleansing, after which life either started over again or moved on to a new level of being. According to some stories our world is not the first; several previous ones have been destroyed.

In Hindu, Mayan, Norse, and other mythologies, the Apocalypse was viewed as part of a cycle, implying that afterward life will resume on earth. However, according to many Western stories, the Apocalypse will be the end of earthly existence. [*See also* FLOOD; GHOST DANCE; GREEK CREATION MYTHS; HOPI EMERGENCE; INDIAN MYTHOLOGY; MAYAN CREATION MYTHS; NAVAJO EMERGENCE; NORSE MYTHOLOGY; RAGNAROK, END OF THE WORLD; RUDRA DESTROYS THE WORLD.]

Apollo (ə päl´ ō)   🐚   The son of ZEUS and Leto, Apollo was the Greek god of healing, light, music, and archery. Artemis, the moon goddess, was his twin sister. Apollo represented order and self-knowledge and was the patron of poets. He was sometimes confused with Helios, who drove the sun chariot across the sky. [*See also* GREEK MYTHOLOGY.]

Ares (âr´ ēz)   🐚   The god of war in GREEK MYTHOLOGY, Ares was the son of ZEUS and HERA. Ares was known for his cruelty and even cowardice and was usually hated by gods and mortals alike. During the Trojan War, he supported the cause of Greek heroes favored by the goddess APHRODITE. In ROMAN AND ETRUSCAN MYTHOLOGY, Ares was known as Mars.

Ariadne (ar ē ad´ nē)   🐚   In GREEK MYTHOLOGY, Ariadne was the daughter of King Minos of Crete. She fell in love with the hero THESEUS when he was a prisoner in her father's LABYRINTH, a complicated maze. Ariadne helped Theseus find his way through the maze so that he could kill the Minotaur, a monster that lived in the labyrinth, and escape. [*See also* MONSTERS AND MYTHICAL BEASTS.]

Arthur, King   🐚   In CELTIC MYTHOLOGY, Arthur was a British king and the leader of the Knights of the Round Table. He held court at his impressive castle in a city named Camelot, where the GRAIL QUEST began. Stories about King Arthur may be based on an actual sixth-century warrior or king. [*See also* ARTHURIAN LEGEND; GAWAIN; GUINEVERE; *MABINOGION;* MERLIN.]

Assyrian Mythology
(ə sēr´ ē ən)   🐚   The ancient civilization of Assyria in Mesopotamia shared many myths with its neighbors, the Babylonians; both groups

The god Apollo was said to play a stringed instrument called the lyre.

Arthurian Legend (är thůr´ē ən)

Stories about King Arthur and his Knights of the Round Table were first told in ancient CELTIC MYTHOLOGY. They were probably based on a real British warrior or king who lived in the A.D. 500s. By the ninth century, the stories of Arthur had expanded to include characters with magic powers, such as MERLIN.

In the 1100s and 1200s, Arthurian legends became popular all over Europe as well as in Great Britain. Poets and ballad singers repeated the tales of chivalry, romance, and noble heroes. The Round Table was first mentioned during this time, and the story of Lancelot and GUINEVERE was added to the Arthurian legends. The saga of the knights GAWAIN, Galahad, and Perceval, and their QUEST for the Holy Grail (in many stories, the cup Christ used at the Last Supper) was expanded under the Christian influence of this period.

Like many heroes, Arthur had a secret parentage, a wise teacher, and a magic weapon. As he grew up, the fact that he was the son of a king was kept secret for his own protection. The magician Merlin was his teacher. When he was a young man, Arthur pulled the powerful sword Excalibur from a stone. The deed proved that Arthur was the true king.

Arthur became a great warrior and a wise ruler in the fabled CITY of Camelot. He had the Round Table built so that he and his knights could sit there as equals. But King Arthur's marriage to beautiful young Guinevere led to his downfall. In some stories, Queen Guinevere plotted against Arthur. In others, she did not want to hurt the king, but she fell hopelessly in love with Sir Lancelot.

Arthur was wounded in a final battle. In an apotheosis revealing his supernatural nature, Arthur was taken to the mythical island of Avalon. Stories say that the king will return some day to create a new Camelot. [*See also* QUETZALCOATL.]

were heavily influenced by the earlier Sumerians. The stories found in the *ENUMA ELISH* were told by both the Babylonians and the Assyrians.

At its highest point in the ninth century B.C., Assyrian civilization was the wonder of the age. The most complete version of the epic tale *GILGAMESH* was found in the library of the last great Assyrian king, Assurbanipal (668–627 B.C.).

The Assyrian PANTHEON of deities included MARDUK, the sun god, and TIAMAT, a dragon goddess of the ocean. Like many cultures throughout the world, the Assyrians told a story of a worldwide FLOOD. [*See also* BABYLONIAN MYTHOLOGY; SUMERIAN/BABYLONIAN FLOOD; SUMERIAN MYTHOLOGY; TAMMUZ.]

Athena (ə thē´ nə) ➤ A goddess of wisdom in GREEK MYTHOLOGY,

The goddess Athena was the subject of many ancient sculptures, including this one from the 700s B.C.

Athena was born from the head of ZEUS, fully grown and armed. Athena supported the arts and crafts and tried to get the Greeks to settle disputes peacefully. When necessary, she could also be a powerful goddess of war. [*See also* ARES.]

Attis (a´ tis) ☞ GREEK MYTHOLOGY includes several versions of the story of Attis, a fertility god. In most stories, he was a Phrygian shepherd and the son and beloved of CYBELE. Attis cas-

trated himself and died beneath a pine TREE, which represented winter or death. Violets (representing spring or rebirth) sprang up from his blood. His resurrection was celebrated every spring. [*See also* DYING GOD; FERTILITY MYTHS; REBIRTH AND RESURRECTION.]

Australian Aboriginal Mythology (ȯ strāl´ yǝn ab ǝ rij´ ǝ nǝl) ☞ The Aborigines were the first inhabitants of Australia. Although their myths vary greatly from place to place, most involve the concept of Dreamtime. In Dreamtime, living Aborigines experience a mythic past, tapping into the stories of their ancestors. Ritually retold in songs, paintings, and drama, these stories provide wisdom essential to the everyday life of Aborigines. On "Walkabouts," Aborigines travel to different sacred places, retracing the travels of their ancestors.

One Aboriginal story called the Seven Sisters explains the origin of the Pleiades constellation (also named the Seven Sisters after seven Greek nymphs). The seven Aboriginal girls put themselves through severe tests and trials. They withdrew from life's comforts and overcame pain, fear, and their own appetites. The Great Spirit was so pleased that he sent the girls to the heavens, where they still appear as the stars in the Pleiades. [*See also* ANCESTOR WORSHIP; DJANGGAWUL DREAMING CREATION; DREAMING; JOURNEY QUEST; SHAMANS.]

B

Baal Myths (ba´ əl) ✎ An early Semitic (Middle Eastern) god of agriculture, weather, and fertility, Baal had a voice like thunder. He struggled constantly against CHAOS, which sometimes took the form of a DRAGON. When Baal was imprisoned in the Underworld, his sister rescued him and fertility returned to the land. [*See also* DYING GOD; FERTILITY MYTHS; UNDERWORLD, DESCENT TO.]

Babylonian Mythology (bab ə lō´ nē ən) ✎ The Babylonian civilization of Mesopotamia thrived, in one form or another, from before 2000 until 539 B.C. The Babylonians took much of their mythology from an earlier people, the SUMERIANS, including the goddess INANNA-ISHTAR and the hero Gilgamesh. The story of APHRODITE AND ADONIS, found in the mythology of the Greeks and Romans, also has Babylonian roots.

The most important source of Babylonian myths is the CREATION epic *ENUMA ELISH*. It tells the stories of such figures as TIAMAT and MARDUK and gives an account of a great FLOOD.

[*See also GILGAMESH*; SUMERIAN/BABYLONIAN FLOOD; TAMMUZ.]

Balder (bȯl´ dər) ✎ In NORSE MYTHOLOGY, Balder was the gentlest and most beautiful of the Scandinavian gods. The son of ODIN, Balder was the best loved of the Aesir, the gods who lived in Asgard. [*See also* BALDER, DEATH OF; ODIN.]

Beowulf (bā´ ə wŭlf) ✎ *Beowulf* was the earliest English-language story about a great hero. The story was written down in the form of a long poem, in about A.D. 1000, although it had been composed hundreds of years earlier. The tale is about the warrior Beowulf, who wanted to be a hero. He went to Denmark, where a monster named GRENDEL had killed many warriors. In a terrible underwater battle, Beowulf killed both the monster and its mother. Beowulf then returned home and became king of his own people, the Geats. When an angry dragon attacked his kingdom, Beowulf fought and killed it, but he was mor-

Information about the preservation of dead bodies was an important part of the *Book of the Dead.*

Death of Balder (bol´ dər)

According to NORSE MYTHOLOGY, the young god BALDER had terrible nightmares that his life was in danger. The other gods worried about his safety.

Balder's mother, FRIGG, went to talk with all natural things. Birds, fire, water, plants, serpents, stones, and trees all promised not to harm Balder. But Frigg missed a little vine, the mistletoe.

Balder's father, ODIN, went to the Underworld to find out who would kill his son. To his surprise the goddess Hel told him that it would be Hoder, Balder's blind twin brother. Meanwhile, the other gods had a great time throwing stones and weapons at Balder. They thought it was wonderful that nothing would hurt him.

LOKI, the TRICKSTER god, was not happy about all this. Disguising himself as a woman, he tricked Frigg into admitting that she had not gotten a promise from the mistletoe. Loki then made a dart from a mistletoe stalk, handed it to Hoder, and guided the blind man's hand as he threw it at Balder. The mistletoe dart killed Balder.

When Odin returned from the Underworld, he was grief stricken to find Balder dead. Another Norse god, Hermod the Bold, rode to the Underworld to see if anything could be done. Hel promised him that if every single thing in the world wept for Balder, he could return to life.

After Balder's funeral, Hermod told the other gods about Hel's promise. Joyfully, they spread the news around the world. But one ogress—a hideous female giant—refused to weep, so Balder had to stay in the Underworld. When the gods discovered that the ogress was Loki in disguise, they chained him to a rock. Odin realized that Balder's death was a sign that Ragnarok, or the end of the world, was drawing nearer. [*See also* RAGNAROK, END OF THE WORLD; UNDERWORLD, DESCENT TO.]

tally wounded in the battle and died soon after. [*See also* MONSTER SLAYING.]

Book of the Dead 🐚 The major source for EGYPTIAN MYTHOLOGY is called the *Book of the Dead.* This collection of ancient texts includes songs, prayers, and magic spells to protect the soul on its journey to the Underworld, as well as information about mummification. [*See also* AFTERLIFE; OSIRIS.]

Brahma (brä´ mə) 🐚 The three creator gods in Hindu INDIAN MYTHOLOGY are Brahma, VISNU, and SIVA. In some CREATION stories, Brahma emerged from an egg in the PRIMAL WATERS. Brahma turned

Blackfoot Orpheus Myth (ôr´ fē us)

NATIVE NORTH AMERICAN MYTHOLOGY includes stories about people who went to the Underworld to find a loved one. One story comes from the Blackfoot. A man was so sad after his wife died that he decided to go and find her. He set out with no idea where to look, but he dreamed of an old woman who told him which way to go. He dreamed of a second old woman, who helped by bringing one of his relatives from the land of the dead. The woman warned the man to keep his eyes closed at all times.

The ghost relative guided the man along a difficult path surrounded by horrible noises. The man kept his eyes closed and went ahead bravely. They reached the chief ghost, who helped by appealing to some of the dead wife's relatives. The relatives agreed to give the woman back, but they made three rules. The man would have to keep his eyes closed for four days as he and his wife traveled out of the Underworld. When they got home, they would have to cleanse themselves in a sweat lodge, and he could never lose his temper with his wife or strike her.

The young man agreed to these rules. The ghosts gave him a sacred pipe and let his wife go with him. He kept his eyes closed as directed, he and his wife purified themselves, and they then went back to normal life. But one day the man got angry because his wife was slow to do something. He picked up a burning stick and shook it at her. Even though he did not intend to hit her, he had broken his promise not to lose his temper. So she vanished and was gone forever. [*See also* JOURNEY QUEST; "ORPHEUS" THEME; UNDERWORLD, DESCENT TO .]

Brahma took many forms in art, including that of an all-seeing being.

Visnu's dreams into physical reality (much like SPIDER WOMAN and TAWA in the HOPI EMERGENCE story). Brahma created a woman from his own body, and then the pair gave birth to humanity. [*See also* DREAMING.]

Brynhild (brin´ hild)   A heroine of NORSE MYTHOLOGY and GERMANIC MYTHOLOGY, Brynhild was a Valkyrie—a woman warrior who took the worthiest dead warriors from the battlefield to Valhalla, the great hall of ODIN. The *NIBELUNGENLIED* tells the story of her complicated relationship with the hero SIEGFRIED, also known as Sigurd.

C

Calypso (kə lip´ sō) 🌀 In
GREEK MYTHOLOGY and Homer's epic poem the *ODYSSEY*, Calypso was a nymph, or NATURE SPIRIT. When ODYSSEUS was shipwrecked near her island, she fell in love with him and promised to make him immortal if he stayed with her. He refused and Calypso kept him prisoner for seven years. She finally freed him at the command of ZEUS.

Caribbean Mythology (kə
ri´ bē ən) 🌀 The people of the Caribbean region have a rich mythology that blends native stories, European myths, and stories brought to the region by Africans.

A cycle of stories that originated with the Taino Indians begins in two caves on the island of Hispaniola. The Tainos came from one cave, called Jagua after the plant used to make body paint. The rest of humanity came from the other cave, Amayauna. The Tainos first lived in the land of Yaya, the spirit of spirits, who had a magic gourd that produced fish to eat. Twin brothers were eating from it one day when they heard Yaya returning. In their haste to hang up the gourd they dropped and broke it. So much water poured from the broken gourd that the whole earth was covered, and the brothers were swept away to a new island.

The voodoo religion of Haiti is of African origin. It came about when African beliefs became mixed with Roman Catholicism. The stories and rituals of voodoo deal with many different spirits called loas. These spirits are kindly and useful, helping people communicate with the voodoo god Bondye. African stories of the Caribbean frequently feature the TRICKSTER Eshu, or LEGBA. [*See also* AFRICAN MYTHOLOGY.]

Odysseus stayed with Calypso for seven years on her island of Ogygia.

Celtic Mythology (kel´tik)

The ancient people of northwestern Europe, the Celts, left a rich mythological heritage. They were the ancestors of the Irish, Scots, Welsh, Cornish, and natives of the Isle of Man. Celts also lived in Brittany (in present-day France), where stories about the magician MERLIN were first told.

Celtic myths were passed down orally for hundreds of years, and then recorded during the Middle Ages. The goddess DANU and other supernatural beings were said to have lived in Ireland before human beings arrived. Their stories, known as the mythological cycle, are found in the *LEABHAR GABHALA*.

The *Táin Bó Cuáilgne (CATTLE RAID OF COOLEY)* is about conflicts between the warriors of Ulster and their neighbors. It is part of a group of myths called the Ulster Cycle. Legends of the hero FINN AND THE FIANNA are told in the FENIAN CYCLE. Stories about some characters from ARTHURIAN LEGEND, as well as the Mother Goddess RHIANNON, were recorded in the *MABINOGION*. Other Celtic myths, especially about specific locations, are found in the *DINNSHENCHAS*. [*See also* CONLAOCH; CUCHULAIN; GAWAIN; GRAIL QUEST; MIDIR AND ETAIN.]

King Arthur and his Knights of the Round Table became a popular subject of Celtic literature.

Changing Woman

Apache and Navajo myths include stories of Changing Woman, a being that could shift from an infant to a girl, a woman, an old crone, and back again at will. [*See also* GREAT GODDESS; NAVAHO EMERGENCE; NAVAJO TWINS.]

Chaos (kā´ös)

In many different CREATION myths, Chaos was an unorganized emptiness that existed at the beginning of everything. Sometimes it was represented by a god or goddess, a monster, or by the PRIMAL WATERS. [*See also* BABYLONIAN MYTHOLOGY; EGYPTIAN CREATION MYTHS; GREEK CREATION MYTHS; JAPANESE CREATION

Cherokee Creation Myths (cher´ ə kē)

As in many other tales from NATIVE NORTH AMERICAN MYTHOLOGY, Cherokee Indian stories about CREATION began with some creatures already in existence. These first animals lived in the heavens, above the endless PRIMAL WATERS.

When the heavens began to get crowded, the first animals looked for someplace else to live. A water beetle was an EARTH DIVER who brought up some mud that expanded into an island. The island floated on the water, and it was fastened to the heavens with four cords. The animals got busy shaping the earth and setting the sun on its regular track. Great Buzzard flapped his wings, creating the mountains and valleys. When the earth was ready, the animals and plants all moved down to it.

A human brother and sister were with the animals. At first, the woman gave birth to a child every seven days. When it seemed that the earth might become crowded, her reproductive cycle changed to once a year.

After a time, the Sun grew angry with the earth people because they squinted their eyes and made faces when they looked at her. The Sun killed many people, and the people fought back by sending Rattlesnake to kill the Sun. But Rattlesnake killed the Sun's daughter by mistake. Then the Sun mourned and refused to come out. The people soothed the Sun with music, and everything returned to normal.

MYTHS; MAYAN CREATION MYTHS; MONSTERS AND MYTHICAL BEASTS; NORSE CREATION MYTHS; TIAMAT.]

Chinese Mythology 🐦

The ancient and varied culture of China has produced a large body of myths about thousands of gods and goddesses, as well as many heroes and heroines. The stories describe an even greater number of supernatural animals, plants, and stones. Many Chinese myths and legends sprang from the traditions of Confucianism, Taoism, and Buddhism, the three main religions of China.

Bronze ceremonial vessels, such as this one from ancient China, played an important role in rituals to Chinese dieties.

Chinese Creation Myths

According to CHINESE MYTHOLOGY, the universe began from nothing. The void that first existed was not even CHAOS—it was just emptiness. Eons passed, and the void slowly changed. Eventually the emptiness divided itself into male and female parts. That pair of creative forces produced another pair of forces. All four powers worked together to bring forth PHAN KU, who was the first real individual being. In another version of the story, Phan Ku emerged from a cosmic egg.

Phan Ku was given tools, a hammer and chisel, so that he could continue the act of CREATION. In some stories he carved out the MOUNTAINS and the sky. In others, he carved the entire earth. As Phan Ku worked, both he and the earth grew larger. His head pushed away the sky as his carving grew. When he had finished, the earth was complete, although nothing lived there. Phan Ku died so that his body could go into the earth and cause life to spring forth. His spirit went to the heavens.

Yet another version of the Chinese creation was a typical DISMEMBERMENT myth. In that story Phan Ku was a giant who was killed in order to form our world. His left eye became the Sun and his right eye the Moon. His skull became the heavens. His bones became rocks, his flesh became soil, his blood became water, and his breath became the wind. The insects crawling on his body became human beings. [*See also* SEPARATION OF HEAVEN AND EARTH.]

The many Chinese deities include the mother goddess KUAN YIN, the war god Kuan Ti, the kitchen god Tsao Chun, and the first being, PHAN KU. One of the oldest Chinese myths is a FLOOD story from about 1000 B.C. For nine years a man named Kun labored to dam up the raging waters that threatened the land. When Kun failed he was executed, and his son Yu took over the job. With the help of a winged dragon, Yu developed new channels that drained the rivers to the sea. [*See also* CHINESE CREATION MYTHS; GREAT GODDESS; HERO AND HEROINE.]

The ancient Greek vase shows Circe, the beautiful woman who bewitched Odysseus and his men.

Cattle Raid of Cooley

The oldest heroic epic in Western Europe is the *Cattle Raid of Cooley* (or *Táin Bó Cuáilgne* as it is called in the Celtic language). First written down in the seventh century, the tale was also included in an early twelfth-century Irish manuscript called the *Book of the Dun Cow*. The story describes a conflict between Ulster and one or more neighboring provinces.

A landowner of Ulster had a great bull named Donn Cuáilgne. The animal was so huge that it could shelter 100 warriors from the heat and cold. Fifty children could play on its back at once. Donn Cuáilgne could father 50 calves a day, and they would all be born the following day. According to some stories the origin of this bull, and another equally grand, went back to two wizards. At various times these wizards took the form of ravens, water beasts, human champions, demons, and water worms. When they were demons, they were swallowed by two cows, then reborn as the finest bulls in Ireland.

Queen Medb of Connacht was jealous because her husband owned one of the bulls. She brought her troops against the Ulstermen to get one, Donn Cuáilgne, for herself. She knew well that an ancient curse gave her an advantage.

According to that story, long ago a husband had boasted that his wife Macha could run faster than the king's horses. Even though she was pregnant, the men forced Macha to race. She gave birth to twins immediately after she won, but she cursed all Ulstermen. Macha's curse caused the weakness of a woman in childbirth to come upon Ulster's warriors in their times of greatest need.

The only warrior who could stand against the curse was CUCHULAIN, who was half god. He ambushed and killed Medb's warriors until she stopped her advance. Then he agreed to meet one of her warriors in single combat each day. Despite Cuchulain's efforts, Medb managed to capture the bull. Finally the Ulstermen shook off the effects of the curse and helped Cuchulain drive the invaders out. During the battle, Cuchulain had to fight and kill his own foster brother, Ferdiad, who had joined Medb's forces. [*See also* CELTIC MYTHOLOGY.]

Circe (sėr´ sē) ☙ In GREEK MYTHOLOGY, Circe was the beautiful daughter of the sun god Helios. Skilled in magic or witchcraft, she lived on an island and put spells on anybody who landed there. The Greek hero ODYSSEUS overcame Circe's magic and rescued his men, whom she had turned into pigs after they landed on her island. [*See also* ODYSSEY.]

City ☙ Real and mythical cities came to represent more than just a

Adventures of Coyote (kī ōt´ē)

COYOTE was a popular TRICKSTER in NATIVE NORTH AMERICAN MYTHOLOGY, especially that of the Plains Indians. He was a mischief-maker and often in trouble himself. Coyote was sometimes killed in his adventures, but he always came to life again.

In a popular Sioux story, Coyote covered a pretty rock with his blanket to keep it warm; he later got cold and took the blanket back. The angry rock rolled along after Coyote and his friend INKTOMI (Spider), chasing them through the woods and even across a river. When it caught up with Coyote, the rock smashed him flat. A rancher who found Coyote took him home to use for a rug. But the next morning, the rug came back to life and ran off.

In some Native American stories, Coyote gave people weapons and places to live and taught them crafts. He also stole fire and gave it to human beings. Once, while visiting the fire people, he sneaked close to their fire and set his headdress aflame. He then ran away and passed the fire on to a relay of other animals. Coyote finally hid the fire in a tree, which is why people can still make fire from sticks of wood.

Some Indian peoples considered Coyote the creator of the world and of human beings. In some EARTH DIVER stories, it was Coyote who created the land. In a Crow Indian story, Coyote made people out of the mud. In a Wasco Indian story, he stranded some bears and wolves in the sky, creating the Big Dipper and the Milky Way. In a Zuni Indian story, Coyote stole the sun and moon, but they escaped from him and ran away to the sky—where they remain today. [See also ZUNI CREATION MYTHS.]

material reality to ancient people. They became identified with specific ideas and points of view. The fall of a city was a great tragedy. In the fall of Troy described in the AENEID, order gave way to chaos. Cities such as Rome, Athens, and Camelot embodied the idea of change from barbarism to civilization. Others, such as Jerusalem, became symbols of the cultures themselves, often reflecting the struggle between people with different concepts of civilization. In some myths, a city represented an order provided by deities or a place where the gods lived before human beings even appeared. [See also AENEAS; ARTHURIAN LEGEND; BABYLONIAN MYTHOLOGY; GREEK MYTHOLOGY; ROMAN AND ETRUSCAN MYTHOLOGY; ROMULUS AND REMUS.]

Conlaoch (con´ lə)

In CELTIC MYTHOLOGY, Conlaoch was the son of CUCHULAIN and a woman warrior named Aoife. He grew up with his mother on the Scottish island of Skye, and when he was grown he went to Ireland to find his father. Before learning the young warrior's name, Cuchulain fought and killed him. In this way, the story is similar to that of the Greek OEDIPUS, except that Oedipus killed his father.

Corn Mother

In many stories from NATIVE NORTH AMERICAN MYTHOLOGY, the Corn Mother spirit (golden-haired in some versions) sacrificed her life when her people could not find food. She directed the people to drag her body over the earth until her skin was gone and then to bury her bones. After they did so, corn grew from her skin and tobacco grew from her bones. [*See also* DISMEMBERMENT; FERTILITY MYTHS; GREAT GODDESS; HAINUWELE; SACRIFICE.]

Coyote (kī ōt´ ē) ☙

Many Native North American peoples tell stories of Coyote, an animal who talked and behaved like a man. He was usually a TRICKSTER and troublemaker. In some stories, however, Coyote was the creator of the world and a great help to human beings. [*See also* COYOTE, ADVENTURES OF; NATIVE NORTH AMERICAN MYTHOLOGY.]

Creation ☙

Stories that explain where everything came from are called creation myths. In some such myths, everything arises from nothingness or from CHAOS. Often the story begins with an existing god, who may create other gods, the earth, humans, and animals. In some creation stories, one or two gods give birth to the world. Others begin with a cosmic egg, PRIMAL WATERS, or the EMERGENCE of gods, people, or animals from within the earth, like children being born. Sometimes a thought or a spoken word brings the world into being.

Creation myths give reasons for our own existence. They often include a story about our FALL FROM GRACE to explain the world's imperfections.

Adventures of Cuchulain (kü hü´ lin)

The Irish hero CUCHULAIN was a major figure in CELTIC MYTHOLOGY, in stories told about the men of Ulster. He was usually said to be the son of Lugh, the god of light, and a mortal queen. From early childhood Cuchulain showed great strength and a warrior's spirit. At age six, he defeated 150 other boys at a form of hockey. At seven he heard a prophecy that those who took up arms on a certain day would be famous but would die young. Determined to be famous, Cuchulain became a warrior on that day. He rushed to southern Ulster, where he defeated and killed three huge brothers who had been killing Ulstermen. At age 17, he was Ulster's only defense during the CATTLE RAID OF COOLEY.

Cuchulain was normally boyish and handsome. But in battle, he went into a frenzy that could be dangerous to anyone nearby. His hair stood on end and light blazed around him. His face was distorted and his body twisted and shook. For the honor of Ulster, he sometimes fought and killed those dear to him, including his foster brother, Ferdiad, and his own son, CONLAOCH.

Cuchulain's supernatural powers were eventually overcome by those of Queen Medb. In his final battle, at age 27, the warrior was tricked into giving up his spears by three warriors who made fun of him. Although he got one spear back and continued fighting, he was wounded and realized that his death was near. Determined to die standing up, Cuchulain tied himself to a post. His great gray horse defended him and was also killed in the battle. Only when a raven landed on Cuchulain's head were his enemies convinced that the mighty warrior was dead. Stories continued to be written about the hero Cuchulain for hundreds of years.

Some creation stories also describe how the world will end, perhaps in an APOCALYPSE. According to some myths, creation is part of an ever-recurring cycle in which worlds arise, are populated, are destroyed, and are replaced by other worlds. [*See also* creation myths of various cultures.]

Cronos (crō´ nəs) 🐚 In GREEK MYTHOLOGY, Cronos was a Titan, the son of URANUS and GAIA. With help from his mother, he led a revolt of the Titans against his father and then assumed rulership of the world. Cronos married his sister Rhea and sired several of the greatest Greek gods. Fearing that he might be overthrown someday by his own children, Cronos swallowed them as infants. But ZEUS later tricked him into disgorging them. ZEUS then led the other gods in overthrowing Cronos. In Roman mythology, Cronos is associated with Saturn, an ancient god who supposedly reigned over Italy during a time of great prosperity. [*See also* HERA; HADES; DEMETER; POSEIDON].

Cuchulain (kü hü´ lin) 🐚 In CELTIC MYTHOLOGY, Cuchulain was a great warrior who had superhuman strength from childhood. He got his name, which means Culann's Hound, after he killed a vicious hound and then guarded its master's livestock while another dog grew up to take its place. Cuchulain won many battles, but he chose fame over long life and died young. [*See also* CUCHULAIN, ADVENTURES OF .]

Cybele (sib´ ə lē) 🐚 A fertility goddess worshiped in Asia Minor, Cybele was the daughter of the king of Phrygia. The king was unwilling to raise a baby girl, so he put her out on a MOUNTAIN to die. Lions, tigers, and other wild beasts recognized that this baby was a deity and nursed her. A shepherd woman then took her home and raised her. As an adult goddess, Cybele sat on a throne flanked by lions, but she remained devoted to the mountain people and to children.

The goddess Cybele is shown here with fertility symbols.

Cupid and Psyche (kyü´ pəd) (sī´ kē)

The son of Venus and MERCURY, Cupid was the god of love in ROMAN AND ETRUSCAN MYTHOLOGY. (Cupid is known as Eros in GREEK MYTHOLOGY.) His magic arrows made gods or mortals fall in or out of love.

Cupid was a handsome young man, and Psyche was the mortal daughter of a king. Psyche was so beautiful that many men wanted to see her. Venus grew jealous of Psyche and asked Cupid to make the young woman fall in love with a monster. But when Cupid saw Psyche, he fell in love with her himself.

Psyche's father became worried because his daughter showed no interest in marriage. He went to the oracle of APOLLO for advice. (An oracle was the shrine of a prophetic deity, who spoke through a priestess. The oracle's advice was usually ambiguous, or unclear.) Apollo knew how Cupid felt, so he told Psyche to wait on a hilltop alone until a DRAGON found her. That dragon would be her husband.

Psyche fell asleep on the hilltop and then woke up inside a palace. She had servants as well as plenty of food and wine. Her husband visited her at night, but he warned her that she must never see him.

Psyche finally became too curious about her husband's appearance. While he lay asleep in the dark, she lighted a lamp and a drop of hot oil woke him. To her surprise, her mysterious husband was Cupid. Burned with the hot oil, Cupid fled and the heartbroken Psyche went on a search for him. She sought the help of Venus, who gave Psyche difficult tasks that included going to the Underworld. Venus then put Psyche into a deep sleep, but Cupid found her and woke her.

Cupid sought permission from JUPITER to marry Psyche. He agreed and made Psyche immortal. The god announced that the couple was married, so Venus had to leave them alone. [*See also* APHRODITE; UNDERWORLD, DESCENT TO.]

The wife of the god Saturn, she fell in love with her son, ATTIS, who killed himself out of madness. She mourned him ever after. In ROMAN AND ETRUSCAN MYTHOLOGY, Cybele was known as the Great Mother. [*See also* FERTILITY MYTHS; GREAT GODDESS.]

Cyclopes (sī klō´ pēz) 🐚 In GREEK MYTHOLOGY, the Cyclopes were a race of one-eyed giants. The first three of their kind were born to URANUS and GAIA. They labored for the god HEPHAESTUS. A community of man-eating Cyclopes later lived on the the island of Sicily, where they menaced heroes such as ODYSSEUS and AENEAS. [*See also* GREEK CREATION MYTHS; MONSTERS AND MYTHICAL BEASTS.]

Danu (da´nü) 🐚 In CELTIC MYTHOLOGY, Danu was the mother of the gods. She is sometimes also known as Dana or Don.

According to ancient Irish stories, Danu and other supernatural beings lived in Ireland before human beings did. Although Danu's people were defeated by human invaders, they are said to be among the ancestors of the current inhabitants. Danu appears in the *LEABHAR GABHALA*.

Danu was also the name of a goddess in INDIAN MYTHOLOGY. In the *RIG VEDA*, the Hindu goddess Danu represented the PRIMAL WATERS. Her name meant restraint. One of her sons, a demon named Vritra, battled with the god INDRA and lost. When Indra destroyed Vritra, he also killed Danu, releasing the primal waters that the pair had restrained. Then the waters were available to complete the CREATION. [*See also* GREAT GODDESS; MONSTERS AND MYTHICAL BEASTS.]

Dausi Epic (dä ü´ sē) 🐚 In AFRICAN MYTHOLOGY, the *Dausi* epic dates back to 500 B.C. According to the epic, the goddess Wagadu represented the strength in human hearts.

It was said that she often could be heard and seen. But whenever she became exhausted by human faults, she fell asleep and disappeared for a long time.

The first time Wagadu vanished was because of the vanity of a warrior named Gassire. Eager for fame, Gassire longed to compose a battle song called the *Dausi*. But his lute could not make music because it had no heart. Gassire thought the lute needed to experience battle, so he carried it with him whenever he fought. When several of his sons died in battle, he fed the lute their blood. However, the lute still would not sing.

Eventually, Gassire's people grew tired of war and asked him to leave. After he went away to the desert, his lute finally sang the *Dausi*. Overwhelmed by the song, Gassire wept. At that moment Wagadu disappeared and did not reappear for a very long time.

Wagadu has come and gone several times since then. She has not reappeared since the last time she fell asleep. But one day she will return, and then she will be so strong that she will never vanish again.

Ceres, the counterpart of the Greek goddess Demeter, is shown holding stalks of wheat.

After falling in love, Dido and Aeneas told each other about their troubles.

Demeter (di mēt´ ər) 🕭 In GREEK MYTHOLOGY, Demeter was the corn goddess, responsible for all crops and vegetation. She was the sister of ZEUS and the mother of PERSEPHONE. Her rites were celebrated in the Greek city of Eleusis and were known as the Eleusinian Mysteries. In ROMAN AND ETRUSCAN MYTHOLOGY, Demeter was known as Ceres. [*See also* FERTILITY MYTHS; GREAT GODDESS; PERSEPHONE, HADES, AND DEMETER.]

Dido (dī´ dō) 🕭 In ROMAN AND ETRUSCAN MYTHOLOGY, Dido was the founder and queen of Carthage, a CITY in northern Africa. Virgil's *AENEID* tells how Venus, the goddess of love, caused her to fall in love with AENEAS. When Aeneas abandoned her, Dido killed herself.

Dikithi (dē kē´ thē) 🕭 In the mythology of the Bantu of Africa, animals and people alike were in awe of the TRICKSTER Dikithi. They called him "The Great Dikithi" because he was such an excellent thief.

Dikithi did not get along well with his mother-in-law. He killed her, but she came back to haunt him until he finally finished her off for good by setting fire to her. He made a whistle out of her leg bone. Dikithi also murdered his father, and invited his friends to feast on the contents of the old man's stomach. [*See also* AFRICAN MYTHOLOGY.]

Dinnshenchas (din hen´ cus) 🕭 *The History of Places*, or *Dinnshenchas* (also *Dindsenchas*), tells stories about the hills, rivers, fords, lakes,

Deeds of Dionysus (dī ō nī´ sus)

Stories about Dionysus appear in the Homeric hymns, the works of the ancient historians Hesiod and Plutarch, and in ancient Greek plays.

ZEUS' wife, the goddess HERA, became furiously jealous of Semele and had her killed before Dionysus was born. Zeus quickly snatched the unborn child and stitched him into his own thigh. Dionysus was safe there for a time, but after he was born Hera had him torn to pieces. Dionysus was rescued and put back together by his grandmother, the goddess Rhea. To protect the child, Zeus sent him to live among the nymphs, or female NATURE SPIRITS. While he was growing up, Dionysus invented wine.

Hera eventually found Dionysus and drove him mad. He wandered far from home. During his travels, he rescued the princess ARIADNE from the island where THESEUS had abandoned her. Dionysus also went to the Underworld to find his mother, and then he took her to live with the gods on Olympus. After other adventures, Dionysus returned home, and Rhea cured his madness.

Pentheus, the young king of Thebes, disapproved of Dionysus, his wine, and his wild female followers. Angry at the disapproval, Dionysos drove Pentheus mad by sending him to spy on the bacchantes, who were Dionysus' followers. Led by Pentheus' own mother, the bacchantes mistook the king for a lion and tore him to pieces.

Eventually, Dionysus was accepted in his homeland and worshiped with the other Olympian deities. His powers included the ability to change into a bull, a serpent, or a lion. He also could turn sticks into deadly weapons. Some Greek myths say that Dionysus died a painful death every year when the grapevines died; he then returned to life in the spring. [*See also* DISMEMBERMENT; DYING GOD; PERSEPHONE, HADES, AND DEMETER; REBIRTH AND RESURRECTION; UNDERWORLD, DESCENT TO.]

and other features in the Irish landscape and how they got their names. Written down in the twelfth century, it is an important source of CELTIC MYTHOLOGY.

Dionysus (dī ō nī´ sus)

The god of wine in GREEK MYTHOLOGY, Dionysus (or Dionysos) was the only half-mortal in the Olympian PANTHEON. He was the son of the god ZEUS and the mortal woman Semele. [*See also* DIONYSUS, DEEDS OF.]

Dismemberment

Myths from many cultures describe the dismemberment, or cutting up, of a god or monster, often as part of a CREATION story. In NORSE CREATION MYTHS, the earth was made from the

The god Dionysus was known as Bacchus by the Romans.

eyebrows of the giant YMIR. In BABY-LONIAN MYTHOLOGY the body of the chaos giantess TIAMAT became the earth and heavens. [*See also* ANIMISM; DIONYSUS; HAINUWELE; OSIRIS; QUETZAL-COATL SAGA; RIG VEDA CREATION.]

Dragons

Huge reptilelike creatures with wings, claws, and large teeth have been described in myths from around the world. These dragons breathed fire or poison and had scales like armor—though they also had some vulnerable spots.

Dragons often guarded fabulous treasures. Some demanded human sacrifices (usually a beautiful princess).

Djanggawul Dreaming Creation
(di jäng´ ə wūl)

In AUSTRALIAN ABORIGINAL MYTHOLOGY, Djanggawul and his two sisters created the features of our world. Before the CREATION, there was a period referred to as "the time of the dreaming," when the earth was empty and desolate. The sun and moon, along with many supernatural beings, still slept beneath the ground. At the beginning of creation, all woke from their sleep. The sun rose from beneath the earth into the sky to warm those new creatures that emerged. Some of the newly created beings took the form of plants or animals; others became humans.

Djanggawul and his sisters appeared on the earth in human form, and they lived on an island far out at sea. They traveled to the mainland of Australia in a bark canoe, overcoming many difficulties along the way. When they landed, Djanggawul plunged his walking stick into the sand and a spring gushed forth. The three then went across Australia, naming the animals and places. They taught human beings language and instructed them how to live.

After they had crossed all of Australia, Djanggawul tripped and accidentally stabbed his walking stick deep into the sand. So much water rushed out that the land was flooded, separating a piece of land from the rest of Australia. This became known as Elcho Island. Eventually the brother and sisters returned to their original island.

The story of Djanggawul and his sisters is told in a cycle of 188 songs. [*See also* BRAHMA; DREAMING.]

Dogon Creation Myths (dō´ gän)

The Dogon people of Mali told a CREATION story similar to that of the general Mande culture of which they were a part. According to Dogon myth, the world began with a cosmic egg. The universe stirred seven times, shaking the great egg and dividing the life inside it into two birth sacs. A set of male and female twins grew in each sac. Their father was the highest deity, AMMA.

One male twin, Yoruga, broke out of his sac before he was scheduled to be born. A piece of the sac tore loose and formed the earth. When Yoruga found himself alone in the universe, he tried to return for his twin. But she had been moved to the other sac with the other pair. So Yoruga went to join the Earth, his mother.

People were created later, when Amma sent the twins and the one from the first sac to the earth. They became the ancestors of the human race.

Westerners first heard about many Dogon myths from Ogotemmeli, a Dogon holy man who studied nature and his people's creation stories after being blinded in a hunting accident. His stories were recorded by a French anthropologist in the early 1900s. [*See also* AFRICAN MYTHOLOGY.]

Annoyed dragons attacked human settlements, burning buildings and killing the inhabitants. Many of the heroes in English, European, and GREEK MYTHOLOGY were dragon-slayers. In Asian myths, however, dragons were usually kindly, and the Chinese dragon kings were gods of the earth's waters. [*See also* BAAL MYTHS; *BEOWULF*; CUPID AND PSYCHE; JASON AND THE GOLDEN FLEECE; SACRIFICE; SIEGFRIED; TIAMAT.]

Draupadi (drou´ pə dē) 🐚 The

story of Princess Draupadi is told in INDIAN MYTHOLOGY and recorded in the *MAHABHARATA*. She became the wife of five brothers, the PANDAVAS, because their mother had declared that her sons must share everything. When the brothers wagered Draupadi in a dice game, they lost. But Draupadi refused to honor the results. She said that her husbands were slaves, and therefore could not make bets. The winner of the game angrily tried to have Draupadi stripped of her clothes, but she prayed to KRISHNA, who helped her. Whenever anyone pulled Draupadi's clothes off, new clothes appeared. Finally she walked scornfully from the hall, still fully dressed, and followed by her five humbled husbands.

Dreaming 🐚 AUSTRALIAN ABO-

RIGINAL MYTHOLOGY describes a

mythic past called Dreamtime. Dreaming refers to an individual's own ancestry that is traced back to one of the Dreamtime gods. The Aborigines use elaborate ritual dances, songs, paintings, and stories to reconnect themselves with their mythic past. Part of their personal Dreaming is the "Walkabout," a JOURNEY QUEST during which they follow the tracks of their ancestors. [*See also* ANCESTOR WORSHIP; BRAHMA; DJANGGAWUL DREAMING CREATION.]

Durga (dôr´gə) 🪶 In INDIAN
MYTHOLOGY, the GREAT GODDESS Devi had many different forms. One of these, Durga, was known as "the inaccessible" one. She was described as a fierce and aggressive goddess, famous for fighting and destroying demons. She had eight or ten arms, golden skin, and was usually seen riding a lion or tiger. In later Hindu traditions, however, Durga was seen as a gentle mother goddess, identified with fertility and standing for family unity. Her story is told in the *MAHAB-HARATA*, the *RAMAYANA*, and the *RIG VEDA*. [*See also* FERTILITY MYTHS; KALI; MONSTER SLAYING; MONSTERS AND MYTHICAL BEASTS; PARVATI.]

Dying God 🪶 In myths from
many cultures, a god-king connected with agricultural cycles had to die and be reborn—often every year. Such stories often included going to the Underworld and returning to the earth's surface. On earth, the seasons

The Buffalo Demon was one of the many beasts killed by the goddess Durga.

changed accordingly, as they did in the story of PERSEPHONE, HADES, AND DEMETER. Sometimes the dying god was a scapegoat who took upon himself the sins of his people. The death and rejuvenation cycle could also be related to the spiritual rebirth of a people. [*See also* ADONIS; ATTIS; BAAL MYTHS; DIONYSUS; FERTILITY MYTHS; OSIRIS; UNDERWORLD, DESCENT TO.]

Earth Diver

Earth Diver According to many CREATION stories in NATIVE NORTH AMERICAN MYTHOLOGY, an earth diver helped give the other animals a place to live. The world was covered by water, so a TRICKSTER god asked for some earth. The dive for it was very dangerous; several creatures tried but failed.

Finally a good swimmer returned, half-dead but clutching a bit of mud. In different versions of the story, the successful earth diver was Beaver, Crawfish, Loon, Mink, Muskrat, or Turtle. The trickster god magically increased the mud, collected by the earth diver, creating all the land. [*See also* CHEROKEE CREATION MYTHS; LONE MAN AND THE MANDAN CREATION; PRIMAL WATERS; SKY GIRL.]

Eddas (ed´əs) The major sources for NORSE MYTHOLOGY are the *Poetic Edda* and the *Prose Edda*. The *Poetic Edda*, or *Elder Edda*, is a collection of Icelandic poems from about the tenth century A.D. The poems tell the ancient stories of Norse gods, heroes, and heroines.

In about A.D. 1220, an Icelandic historian and poet named Snorri Sturluson collected the traditional stories told in Norse myths. He rewrote them in prose (ordinary writing without the metrical patterns of poetry) and published them as the *Prose Edda*, or *Younger Edda*. Sturluson reinterpreted many of the old myths from a Christian perspective—for example, making the TRICKSTER god LOKI into a darker character than did earlier Icelandic poems. [*See also* GERMANIC MYTHOLOGY.]

The Icelandic Eddas include stories about the creation of the world.

Egyptian Creation Myths

The story of CREATION was told several different ways in ancient EGYPTIAN MYTHOLOGY. In the oldest stories, the female principle Nun, or CHAOS, was the primal ocean from which all things came. Nun gave birth to Atum, who in turn created the universe. Other stories simply began with PRIMAL WATERS and the first deity, the sun, which was sometimes pictured as an eye. The Sun God—RA, Atum, Atum-Ra, or Ptah—brought order and created the universe. Ptah was said to have created the other gods and everything in the universe from ideas in his own mind.

In another version of the creation story, the universe was made by two deities who were the children of Shu (the brother of Ra). Geb was the Earth God who lay flat. Nut was the Sky Goddess who arched over him. When they parted, they produced the universe. GEB AND NUT gave birth to the first god-king OSIRIS, his wife ISIS, and the people of Egypt.

Egyptian creation myths include several examples of brothers and sisters as cocreators or WORLD PARENTS. The pharaohs, or Egyptian rulers, supported this practice of marriage between brothers and sisters, believing that it kept their divine lineage pure. [*See also BOOK OF THE DEAD*; BRAHMA; HORUS; OSIRIS, DEATH AND RESURRECTION OF; SETH; TAWA.]

Egyptian Mythology

Egypt's long-lasting and ancient culture produced an elaborate system of myths. They described CREATION, the relationships of numerous deities, the development of a civilization led by pharaohs (divine kings), and ways of gaining immortality in the AFTERLIFE. All things in the world were thought to be capable of supernatural power. Many Egyptian deities could take animal form, and certain creatures (including cats and scarab beetles) were considered sacred. [*See also BOOK OF THE DEAD*; EGYPTIAN CREATION MYTHS; GEB AND NUT; HORUS; ISIS; OSIRIS; RA; SETH.]

The *Book of the Dead* contained many stories about creation.

Emergence

NATIVE NORTH AMERICAN MYTHOLOGY includes many CREATION stories in which people and other living things first emerged from a place deep within the earth. According to such myths, creatures and plants developed and grew in the darkness below. When they were mature enough, they came out into the daylight by way of a cave or a hole in the ground. This was like the birth of a child from its mother's womb. Sometimes a deity such as SPIDER WOMAN in myths of the southwestern United States, helped with the birth.

Such stories vary from one Native American culture to the next. Similarly, according to the Australian DJANGGAWUL DREAMING CREATION story, the sun, moon, supernatural

Native Americans often buried pottery with the dead to represent the connection between birth and death, or an emergence to a new form.

beings, and people all emerged from beneath the earth. In other creation myths from around the world, human beings or deities emerged from a cosmic egg. [*See also* ACOMA CREATION MYTH; APACHE CREATION MYTHS; HOPI EMERGENCE; KIOWA CREATION MYTHS; NAVAJO EMERGENCE; ZUNI CREATION MYTHS.]

Enki (en´kē)

The Sumerian deity Enki was the god of the earth's waters, of learning, and of wisdom. Enki brought order to the universe. He created human beings from clay and he saved them when the god Enlil flooded the earth. It was also Enki, however, who turned human speech into many different languages because he was jealous of Enlil.

Enki rescued the goddess Inanna from the Underworld. According to one story, while Enki was drunk, Inanna talked him into giving her many decrees, which she in turn gave to the Sumerians. These became their laws. [*See also* INANNA AND THE UNDERWORLD; INANNA-ISHTAR; SUMERIAN/BABYLONIAN FLOOD; UNDERWORLD, DESCENT TO.]

Enuma Elish (en ü´ma el´esh)

Sometimes known in English as *War of the Gods*, the *Enuma Elish* is one of the world's oldest written CREATION myths. The epic poem was composed in or before the twelfth century B.C. It is an important source of BABYLONIAN MYTHOLOGY. The *Enuma Elish* tells about the creation of the universe, the appearance of the gods, the death of the goddess TIAMAT, the rise of MARDUK to the top of

The ancient Romans often copied earlier Greek art. This Roman sculpture shows Eurydice with Orpheus and Hermes.

This painting from the Middle Ages shows Adam and Eve (at the left) being expelled from the Garden of Eden.

the PANTHEON of gods, and the creation of humankind.

Etiology (ēt ē äl´ ə jē) 🐦 The study of the origins of things is called etiology. Many myths explain the origins of specific things, such as the appearance and behavior of human beings, animals, and insects; why there is day and night or death; and why the seasons change. These are etiological myths.

Eurydice (yü rid´ ə sē) 🐦 In GREEK MYTHOLOGY, Eurydice was a beautiful woman loved by the masterful musician and poet ORPHEUS. She died from a snakebite soon after

their wedding, and Orpheus vainly attempted to rescue her from the Underworld. [*See also* ORPHEUS AND EURYDICE.]

Eve (ēv´) 🐦 According to the Hebrew CREATION stories told in the book of Genesis in the Bible, Eve was the first woman. In one version of the story, God created Eve from the rib of the first man, ADAM. The couple lived in the Garden of Eden but were expelled after they ate fruit that God had forbidden them to eat. They were the parents of the human race. [*See also* GREAT GODDESS; *LEABHAR GABHALA*; LILITH; NAVAJO EMERGENCE; PANDORA; SKY GIRL.]

F

Fall from Grace ◈ The myths of many cultures tell of a beautiful paradise that human beings once lived in but were forced to leave. At first deities watched over humans and met their needs. But through some character flaw or disobedience, humans found themselves in a harsher world. According to some stories, all experienced a fall from grace because of the actions of one or two people. In GREEK MYTHOLOGY, for example, the gods gave PANDORA a box that she was never to open. When her curiosity led her to disobey, she released evil into the world and the golden age was over. In a biblical story, ADAM and EVE were expelled from the Garden of Eden because they ate a forbidden fruit, and all their descendants were banned from this garden paradise. Stories in Jewish and Islamic traditions also mention angels who fell from grace.

Faro (fär´ ō) ◈ In the CREATION myth of the Mande of Africa, Faro was a male twin, one of two pairs of twins who grew in a cosmic egg. The other male twin, Pemba, left the egg early. Pemba's actions resulted in the creation of the earth, but he was an incom-

plete being. In order to start the creation over, the high god Mangala sacrificed Faro and cut him into 60 pieces. Mangala turned the pieces of Faro into TREES on the earth, which represented the idea of REBIRTH AND RESURRECTION. The high god then brought Faro back to life and sent him to earth in an ark. When Mangala flooded the earth to purify it, Faro was responsible for saving some of the plants and animals. [*See also* DOGON CREATION MYTH; FLOOD.]

Father God ◈ In the myths of many cultures, the supreme deity or creator is the Father God. In some stories he and a goddess mated to produce the world and its features, including people. The Father God was most often identified with the Heavens, the Sky, or the Sun. But in EGYPTIAN CREATION MYTHS the father god Geb represented the Earth. In FINNIC CREATION MYTHS the father was the sea. Some father gods, such as the Greek god ZEUS, were not the original creators but ruled over a PANTHEON of deities. In other myths, a supreme deity created both the father and the mother. [*See also* AMMA; APACHE CREATION MYTHS; FROG AND WIYOT; GEB AND

Finn and the Fianna (fin´) (fē a´ nə)

According to the FENIAN CYCLE of CELTIC MYTHOLOGY, the Irish hero Finn MacCumal became a warrior at an early age. In that he was like CUCHULAIN, the hero in stories known as the Celtic Ulster Cycle. Unlike Cuchulain, Finn lived a long, rich life and did not fight his battles alone. His band of heroic warriors and hunters, called the Fianna, always traveled with him.

A man who wished to join the Fianna had to pass severe TRIALS AND TESTS. With only a shield and a stick, he had to fend off spears cast by nine warriors. He had to escape the other Fianna in a chase through the forest. If he was wounded or captured in any of the tests, the man was rejected. Those who became Fianna were dedicated to their leader and the group. Where the hero stories of the Ulster cycle emphasized individualism and competition, those about the Fianna demonstrated fellowship.

Finn and the Fianna had many adventures together. When Finn was a famous mature warrior, they faced a particularly difficult romantic situation. Finn planned to marry Grainne, the young daughter of King Cormac. Grainne respected the warrior, but did not want to be his wife. She used magic to make a young Fianna named Diarmuid fall in love with her and help her slip away. For years, the couple lived happily in another land, but eventually Grainne longed to see her father and home again. She and Diarmuid invited King Cormac and Finn to a great feast, which went peacefully enough. The next day, Diarmuid joined Finn on a hunt for a great boar. Diarmuid was wounded by the magic beast, which had sought him out because of a family curse. Finn hesitated too long to use his own powers of healing to save Diarmuid's life, and the wounded warrior died.

NUT; GREEK CREATION MYTHS; HAWAIIAN CREATION MYTHS; JAPANESE CREATION MYTHS; MAORI CREATION MYTHS; NORSE CREATION MYTHS; ODIN; SEPARATION OF HEAVEN AND EARTH; TAMMUZ; TAWA; WORLD PARENTS; ZUNI CREATION MYTHS.]

Father, Search for ☙

In the myths of many lands, a hero has to solve a mystery surrounding his male parent. The search for the father represents a search for identity, and it often leads out to the discovery of a hero's divinity. In NATIVE NORTH AMERICAN MYTHOLOGY, for example, MANABOZHO found and confronted his father, the West Wind. Similarly, WATERJAR BOY searched for and found his father, even though his mother claimed he had none.

In other stories the father was known but missing. After the Greek hero ODYSSEUS had been away for 20 years, his son Telemachus went searching for him. CONLAOCH, the

Finnic Creation Myth (fin´ik)

The Finnic creation myth is described in traditional songs and in the *KALEVALA*, which includes stories about the PRIMAL WATERS as well as the cosmic egg.

Ilmatar, the air spirit, floated above the endless water. She eventually descended into the sea and was tossed about by the waves. A duck landed on Ilmatar's knee and built a nest there. The duck laid seven eggs, six of gold and one of iron. However, as the duck sat on the eggs, they grew warm and burned Ilmatar's knee. In an effort to cool her knee, she upset the nest and the eggs were broken up by the waves. Part of one eggshell became the land, and another became the sky. The egg yolk became the sun, and the whites became the moon and stars.

Ilmatar gave birth to the first man, VAINAMOINEN, who swam for years until he reached land. He cleared some land to plant seeds but thoughtfully left a tree standing for the birds to use. A grateful eagle gave him fire, so Vainamoinen then burned the fields and planted barley. [*See also* FINNIC MYTHOLOGY.]

his men—a legendary band of Irish warriors called the Fianna—are collected in the Fenian Cycle of CELTIC MYTHOLOGY. Many of the ballads were apparently written by Finn's son Oisin.

Though a warrior, Finn was also a poet with mystical powers. In one story, a man had been stealing food. When Finn jammed his thumb in a door, he put the sore thumb in his mouth and immediately divined the name of the thief and proceeded to kill him. Chewing his thumb magically revealed important information in other stories. Many of Finn's enemies also had supernatural abilities. [*See also* FINN AND THE FIANNA.]

Fertility Myths

Fertility myths were stories of deities and powers that could control the earth's growing cycles, the reproduction of animals, and the birth of children. Early people recognized the importance of reproduction for survival, and some very ancient works of art were apparently connected with fertility magic. Both gods and goddesses were called upon to bring fertility to the land or to people. Sometimes the bodies of these deities were planted, either symbolically or literally, into the earth and sprouted into food crops. Infertility was thought to be due to the anger of a god or goddess. [*See also* ADONIS; ARIADNE; ATTIS; BAAL MYTHS; CORN MOTHER; CYBELE; DEMETER; DYING GOD; FREYA; GEB AND NUT; GREAT GODDESS;

son of the Celtic hero CUCHULAIN, searched for his father, but when Conlaoch refused to identify himself, he was killed. The Trojan hero AENEAS, guided by the SIBYL of Cumae, sought and found his father in the Underworld. [*See also* ARTHURIAN LEGEND; THESEUS.]

Fenian Cycle (fē´nē ən)

Stories about Finn MacCumal and

HAINUWELE; INANNA-ISHTAR; INDRA; KUAN YIN; OSIRIS; PARVATI; RHIANNON; SACRIFICE; TAMMUZ; WORLD PARENTS.]

Finnic Mythology (fin´ik)

Collected in the *KALEVALA*, Finnic myths tell a CREATION story and follow the adventures of the heroes VAINAMOINEN, Ilmarinen, and Lemminkainen and the witch Louhi. At various times, the three heroes all made efforts to marry one of Louhi's daughters. Vainamoinen and Ilmarinen created a magic object called the Sampo for Louhi, and later stole it from her. In her fury, Louhi stole the sun and the moon and sent both a fierce bear and pestilence to the three heroes' home district. Vainamoinen took care of the pestilence and the bear, and Ilmarinen forced Louhi to put back the sun and the moon.

The Finnic myths are set in a mythic place called the Kaleva District. According to the final story of the *Kalevala*, a virgin named Marjatta gave birth to a son. The boy was declared king of the Kaleva District. Furious over this development, Vainamoinen departed, but he left his songs behind for the people. [*See also* FINNIC CREATION MYTHS; LEMMINKAINEN'S DEATH AND RESURRECTION.]

Flood

Myths from many cultures tell of a great flood, or deluge, that nearly destroyed humanity. In most myths, at least two righteous people survived to start the human race over again. The flood was often a punishment from the gods, and afterward the earth and its remaining people were cleansed of evil. Some of these stories are probably based on actual natural disasters. Flood stories represent a cycle of death and rebirth, after which the surviving humans get a fresh start. [*See also* APACHE CREATION MYTHS; APOCALYPSE; FARO; INCAN FLOOD; MANABOZHO; MANU AND THE FISH; MAYAN CREATION MYTHS; MOUNTAIN; NAVAJO EMERGENCE; PROMETHEUS; RUDRA DESTROYS THE WORLD; SUMERIAN/BABYLONIAN FLOOD.]

Freya (frā´ə)

The goddess of love in NORSE MYTHOLOGY, Freya was

This pendant representing Freya shows her wearing a necklace made for her by the dwarves.

Frog and Wiyot (wē´ ät)

The story of Frog and WIYOT, the god who created her, is a common one in NATIVE NORTH AMERICAN MYTHOLOGY. In some versions, Frog was a SHAMAN; in others she was a god's daughter. One of the best-known myths was told by the Luiseño and Gabrielino Indians of California.

According to that story, the god Wiyot was the creator of the world and the father of the people. Frog hated him; she was angry because Wiyot had given her such strange-looking legs. One day Frog sneaked up and spat her poison into Wiyot's drinking water. After the god drank the poison, he realized that he was going to die.

Wiyot told his people that he would die in the spring. Like OSIRIS in EGYPTIAN MYTHOLOGY, as well as many other Native North American characters, Wiyot made sure that his people learned everything they needed to know. He spent the entire winter teaching them how to live on the land, and then he died in the spring. After his death, Wiyot became the moon. His people dance and cry out to greet him each night that he visits them. [*See also* DYING GOD; GLOOSCAP; FATHER GOD; LONE MAN AND THE MANDAN CREATION; OLD MAN; OSIRIS, DEATH AND RESSURECTION OF; QUETZALCOATL; SPIDER WOMAN; TREE; WHITE BUFFALO WOMAN.]

a beautiful, young, blond Valkyrie, one of a group of women warriors who searched the battlefield for heroes who had died a noble death. They took those dead warriors to Valhalla, the great hall of the god ODIN. In some stories Freya had her own hall, where she took half of the dead heroes. With her falcon skin cloak, Freya could fly, and she traveled to the Underworld. For a time she was Odin's wife. Friday is named for Freya. [*See also* BRYNHILD; FRIGG; LOKI'S TRICKS.]

Frigg (frig´) The Mother Goddess of NORSE MYTHOLOGY, Frigg was the principal wife of ODIN and the mother of BALDER. Described as very quiet and wise, Frigg was the goddess of the sky and of marriage. She was one of the Aesir, a group of warrior deities who lived in Asgard, one of nine worlds. Frigg was said to help women in childbirth and to enjoy visiting earth and interfering in human lives. In later GERMANIC MYTHOLOGY, FREYA and Frigg were blended into one character. [*See also* BALDER.]

G

Gaia (gī´ə) ☙ In GREEK CREATION MYTHS, Gaia (or Gaea) was Mother Earth—the planet we live on portrayed as a deity. She was born during the early phases of CREATION and is said to have created her husband, URANUS, Father Heaven. Among their many children were the Titans, an early generation of gods. [*See also* GREAT GODDESS; GREEK MYTHOLOGY.]

Ganesa (gä ne´shä) ☙ The god of wisdom and art in INDIAN MYTHOLOGY, Ganesa had four hands and

This bronze sculpture shows Gaia and the mother goddess Thalassa.

Ganesa originally had two tusks, but he lost one when he angrily tore it off to throw it at the moon.

Birth of the Ganges (gan′ jēz)

According to INDIAN MYTHOLOGY, the sacred Ganges River originates in heaven, flowing from the toe of the god VISNU. Once, a king named Bhagiratha pleased the god BRAHMA with his penitence and holiness. Brahma promised to grant the king a wish, and the king requested that the river of heaven, the Ganga, flow to the earth. Brahma agreed, but warned that the weight of the great heavenly river would cut the earth in two. Brahma suggested that the god SIVA could help.

Through his holiness, the king also won Siva's favor. The god allowed the heavenly water to flow onto his own head. Siva's matted and snarled hair broke the force of the current, allowing it to flow down to the Himalayan MOUNTAINS without destroying the earth. So the Ganges still flows to the sea.

The river is personified as the goddess Ganga, the deity of abundance, power, and health. In another version of the story, the reason that Siva allowed the heavenly waters to flow on his head was to break the fall of the goddess Ganga so she would not be hurt. Ganga is also identified with the Milky Way, with a river in the Underworld, and with other earthly rivers.

house. Parvati created a son from the dirt of her own body and set him to guard her front door. When Siva arrived, Ganesa was, remarkably, able to strike him. In the battle that followed, Siva cut off Ganesa's head. Parvati was so furious that she destroyed a million gods and was about to destroy the whole world. Wise men finally quieted her with the promise to have Ganesa revived and given a new head. Siva agreed and instructed that Ganesa should have the head of the first being that came by—which happened to be an elephant with one tusk.

Gawain (gə wān′) In ARTHURIAN LEGEND, Sir Gawain was King

the head of an elephant. He was a popular god whose job was to create obstacles and then remove them. His parents were the god SIVA and the goddess PARVATI.

According to one version of Ganesa's story, Parvati was angry with Siva for so freely entering her

The courageous knight Gawain is shown here with his armor and shield.

Arthur's nephew and the most perfect knight of the Round Table. Along with other knights, Gawain vowed to go on a QUEST for the Holy Grail, the cup that Christ supposedly used at the Last Supper. Gawain is best known from a fourteenth-century tale, *Gawain and the Green Knight*, in which he is faced with severe tests of his chivalry and courage. [*See also* GRAIL QUEST.]

Geb and Nut (geb) (nüt) ▸

In EGYPTIAN MYTHOLOGY, Geb and Nut were the children of the Sun God RA. They were the parents of OSIRIS, ISIS, HORUS, Nepthys, and SETH. Geb was the Earth God and Nut was the Sky Goddess. According to some stories Nut arched over Geb, and then their separation created the universe. [*See also* EGYPTIAN CREATION MYTHS; OSIRIS; SEPARATION OF HEAVEN AND EARTH.]

Germanic Mythology ▸

Scandinavian and Germanic myths have a common origin. Germanic tribes originally lived in what is now southern Scandinavia and northern Germany, later migrating into other parts of Europe and Great Britain. Therefore, the Norse stories of the EDDAS became part of the Germanic tradition. ODIN, BALDER, and the other gods of Asgard—the home of the Norse warrior gods—also appear in Germanic stories. The Valkyries— women warriors who searched the battlefield for heroes who had died

Ghost Dance

In the late 1880s, a Native American prophet named Wovoka began preaching a new religion to the Paiute Indians of the West. According to Wovoka, a new earth would soon descend, putting an end to the old one. The Indian ancestors would return, and so would the rapidly disappearing buffalo herds. Life would be eternally wonderful in this new world. To survive the coming APOCALYPSE, Wovoka instructed Indians to perform a ritual dance called the Ghost Dance.

The Ghost Dance religion spread to other tribes, which added new elements to the religion, including the belief that Wovoka was a messiah or deliverer. Dancing Indians also began wearing "ghost shirts" that were supposed to make them invulnerable to the bullets of white soldiers.

When the religion reached the Oglala Sioux at Pine Ridge, South Dakota, white settlers began to panic. After all, Wokova's predictions were about the destruction of the white world. By 1890, the settlers were afraid that there might soon be an Indian uprising. The soldiers arrested the Sioux chief Big Foot and his band of followers at Wounded Knee, South Dakota, on December 28. The next day, the soldiers massacred approximately 200 Sioux men, women, and children, including Big Foot himself.

After this massacre, most Indians lost faith in the Ghost Dance, partly because many of the slaughtered Sioux had been wearing ghost shirts. The movement soon faded away, although Wovoka himself lived until 1932. [*See also* NATIVE NORTH AMERICAN MYTHOLOGY.]

Adventures of Gilgamesh (gil´ gə mesh)

In BABYLONIAN MYTHOLOGY, Gilgamesh was a cruel and harsh king. When his people prayed to the CREATION goddess Aruru for help, she decided that the king needed a strong friend and companion. The goddess created a wild man named Enkidu and had him tamed. When Gilgamesh met Enkidu, the two competed in a wrestling match. Gilgamesh won, but he admired his opponent's courage and strength. Soon they were best friends.

Gilgamesh and Enkidu had many heroic adventures together. They killed the giant, Humbaba, who guarded the MOUNTAIN where the gods lived. They also cut down Humbaba's sacred grove of cedar trees.

The goddess Ishtar fell in love with Gilgamesh, but he wanted nothing to do with her. He reminded the goddess that she had been unkind to her other lovers. Enkidu even made fun of Ishtar. Furious, the goddess sent the Bull of Heaven to bring destruction to the king's people. Together, Gilgamesh and Enkidu killed the vicious bull.

The exploits of Gilgamesh and Enkidu soon began to annoy the gods. They decided they did not like the influence Enkidu was having on the king, so they sent an illness that killed him. For the rest of his life Gilgamesh missed the company of his friend.

Even though Gilgamesh was part god, he knew that he would die some day. But he longed to live forever, so he set out on a JOURNEY QUEST to gain eternal life for himself. Gilgamesh went to see a man named Utnapishtim, a mortal who had been given immortality by the gods. Utnapishtim promised that if Gilgamesh could stay awake for six days and seven nights, he too would become immortal. But the king was exhausted and soon fell asleep.

Utnapishtim next told Gilgamesh that a bite of a certain sacred plant would give him eternal life. However, the plant only grew at the bottom of the ocean. Gilgamesh dove into the deep water and got the plant, then headed back toward Uruk. On the way Gilgamesh stopped to bathe in a well, then he took a nap. While the king slept, a serpent who lived in the well ate the plant. So Gilgamesh did not become immortal, even though he became a famous king. [*See also GILGAMESH;* INANNA-ISHTAR; SUMERIAN/BABYLONIAN FLOOD.]

noble deaths—were popular figures in German myths as well.

Stories about the hero Sigurd originated in what is now Germany, but they also appear in collections of ancient Scandinavian mythology. Sigurd is called SIEGFRIED in the *NIBELUNGENLIED*, which was written about A.D. 1200 for the royal court of Austria. [*See also* NORSE MYTHOLOGY.]

Gilgamesh (gil´ gə mesh)

The oldest-known epic poem, the *Gilgamesh* tells the story of a Babylonian

Adventures of Glooscap (glüs´ kap)

Unlike most TRICKSTERS, the Algonquin character Glooscap had a human form. He was not a clown, a cheat, or an object of jokes. Instead, he was a creator god, always generous toward humans.

While still a baby, Glooscap killed his brother, Wolf, who had killed their mother. He later killed a frog-monster that was blocking a river to keep the water from everyone. When animals became too dangerous, Glooscap made them smaller and taught them to be peaceful.

At one time, winds and storms along the shore made it impossible for people to fish. Glooscap discovered a huge, ancient bird standing on a point of land and flapping its wings—which was creating the wind. Glooscap broke the bird's wing, then fed the creature while it healed. Because some breeze was needed, he convinced the bird to flap its wings more gently, and then he set it free.

Sometimes Glooscap's companion was Turtle, who played the role of a clown. Another friend was the tiny elf of Summer. Fortunately the elf went along when Glooscap made a journey to the home of Winter. Glooscap fell under the spell of Winter and was frozen stiff. The elf, hidden in the trickster's robes, caused Glooscap to cry. His tears thawed the frozen trickster and the surrounding snow. When Glooscap laughed, summer returned to the land.

Glooscap's many other adventures included riding a whale, rescuing kidnapped friends, and being swept through underground rapids. Like King Arthur in the ARTHURIAN LEGENDS and QUETZALCOATL in NATIVE CENTRAL AND SOUTH AMERICAN MYTHOLOGY, Glooscap finally left the world, but he is expected to return when he is needed. [See also MANABOZHO; MONSTER SLAYING.]

---

king of that name. The most complete version of the poem was written down about 650 B.C., but the story of King Gilgamesh may be as much as 3,000 years older. [See also BABYLONIAN MYTHOLOGY; GILGAMESH, ADVENTURES OF.]

Glooscap (glüs´ kap) ☙ In the NATIVE NORTH AMERICAN MYTHOLOGY of the Algonquin Indians, Glooscap was an all-powerful creator spirit and TRICKSTER. He created the animals and taught human beings how to fish, hunt,

and make babies. According to some stories, Glooscap would grant a wish to anyone who made the long seven-year journey to see him. The wish, however, would come true in unpleasant ways if the wisher was too greedy.

Great Goddess ☙ In world myths dating from the most ancient times, a powerful goddess represented CREATION, care-giving, fertility, and death. She appeared in three aspects: maiden, mother, and crone (or

Grail Quest (grâl)

According to ARTHURIAN LEGEND, the Holy Grail was the cup used by Jesus Christ at the Last Supper. It had once been visible to everyone but had vanished because of the world's evils. The knights of King Arthur's round table vowed to find the Grail and set out on a JOURNEY QUEST for it. The young knight PERCEVAL once saw the Grail, and in some stories Sir GAWAIN did too. However, Sir Galahad was the only one to fully succeed in his quest. After he looked into the Grail, Galahad was carried up to heaven.

A sacred object called the Grail appeared in the Welsh epic *MABINOGION* and in earlier CELTIC MYTHOLOGY. It may originally have been a FERTILITY MYTH image. The Grail was described as a glowing chalice, dish, or cup that provided food and healing to those who touched it. A spear hovered over it, dripping blood from its point into the vessel.

hag). This Mother Goddess, or Earth Mother, had the power of creation and was often identified as the Earth itself. In GREEK MYTHOLOGY she was called GAIA. The Mother Goddess was often paired with a mate, usually identified with the sky or heavens. In those stories, creation was the work of WORLD PARENTS. As humans developed agriculture, the Mother Goddess changed into a deity of planting and harvesting called the Great Goddess. The Native North American CORN MOTHER and the Greek DEMETER were directly connected with the growing seasons. Like many other deities, the Great Goddess was capable of doing both good and harm. [*See also* CHANGING WOMAN; CIRCE; CYBELE; DANU; EVE; FERTILITY MYTHS; FREYA; FRIGG; HAINUWELE; HERA; INANNA-ISHTAR; ISIS; IZANAMI AND IZANAGI; KUAN YIN; OKANAGON MOTHER; PANDORA; RHIANNON; SPIDER WOMAN; TIAMAT; WHITE BUFFALO WOMAN.]

Greek Mythology

More than myths of any earlier civilization, the mythology of classical Greece portrayed recognizably human characters. Even the gods seemed human in their virtues and frailties, their kindnesses and cruelties.

In his *THEOGONY*, the Greek poet Hesiod relates GREEK CREATION MYTHS and tells how gods and mortals appeared. In a time before humans and gods even existed, the universe was CHAOS. The first true gods were the Titans, who were eventually overthrown by their children.

Most Greek myths center on these younger gods, the PANTHEON of Mount Olympus. The king of these gods and the ruler of the heavens was ZEUS. Zeus' long-suffering wife, HERA, was also his sister. Zeus' brother HADES ruled the Underworld, while his other brother POSEIDON ruled the

Greek Creation Myths

According to GREEK MYTHOLOGY, there was only CHAOS before the CREATION. Chaos gave birth to Erebus—the realm of the dead—and also to Night. Night laid an egg and left it in the bosom of Erebus. From the egg was hatched Love, which created Light and Day. Soon Father Heaven (also known as URANUS) and Mother Earth (also known as GAIA) took form.

The first children of Father Heaven and Mother Earth were monsters, including one-eyed giants called CYCLOPES. But Heaven and Earth also gave birth to the Titans, the elder gods. For a very long time, the Titan CRONOS and his sister Rhea ruled the universe.

Cronos learned from a prophecy that one of his children would someday overthrow him. So he ate his children as quickly as they were born—all except ZEUS, whom Rhea hid away. As expected, Zeus rebelled against his father and forced him to disgorge the other five children. Zeus and his siblings warred against the Titans and eventually defeated them.

Zeus and two brothers drew lots, then divided the universe between them. POSEI-DON ruled the ocean; HADES ruled the Underworld; Zeus ruled the sky and all the other gods from Mount Olympus.

When it came time for humans to be created, the task was turned over to the Titan PROMETHEUS and his brother Epimetheus. Prometheus had helped the Olympians against the other Titans and was much trusted by Zeus.

Several races of humankind have lived on Earth since then. The golden race was the first and by far the finest; these wise and virtuous people lived without work, pain, or unhappiness. A silver race followed; these people were less wise, and they had to work the land for food. Then came a brass race of warlike, violent people who caused each other terrible harm. After the brass race came a race of brave, adventurous heroes.

Today's people are the iron race—the worst humans so far; this race is plagued with work and suffering, and it grows worse with every passing generation. It is said that Zeus will someday put an end to the iron race and begin humanity anew. [*See also* APOCALYPSE; MONSTERS AND MYTHICAL BEASTS; WORLD PARENTS.]

sea. Unpopular among both gods and mortals, ARES was the god of war. The lesser-known Hestia was the goddess of the hearth. ATHENA was the goddess of wisdom, crafts, and sometimes war. APOLLO, an archer, was the god of music and healing. The beautiful APHRODITE was the goddess of love. HERMES was the swift-footed messenger god. Artemis, the moon goddess, was a great huntress. The club-footed HEPHAESTUS was the god of the forge. These deities were a quarrelsome group, and their differences often led to trouble for mortals.

Two part-gods who eventually joined the Greek pantheon at Olympus were DIONYSUS (or Bacchus) and HERCULES. The corn goddess DEMETER and her daughter PERSEPHONE were also important deities connected with agricultural cycles.

Greek stories included other gods, mortals, and characters who were children or descendants of both. The most important literary works about these figures are the two epic poems said to have been written by the Greek poet Homer. His *ILIAD* deals with the Trojan war and includes such characters as ACHILLES and HELEN. His *ODYSSEY* relates the wanderings of ODYSSEUS after that war. [*See also* ADONIS; ALCESTIS; ARIADNE; CALYPSO; CIRCE; CUPID AND PSYCHE; CYCLOPS; EURYDICE; GAIA; HECATE; HOMERIC HYMNS; HYACINTHUS; IO; JASON; LEDA; MEDEA; MEDUSA; NARCISSUS; ORPHEUS; PANDORA; PENELOPE; PERSEUS; PROMETHEUS; THESEUS; UNDERWORLD, DESCENT TO; URANUS.]

Grendel (gren´ dəl) 🐾 In the old English poem *BEOWULF*, the monster Grendel had been attacking and devouring the people of Denmark for 12 years. A warrior named Beowulf came from the nearby land of the Geats to help defeat the monster. Beowulf became a hero by killing

Grendel and the monster's mother. [*See also* MONSTER SLAYING.]

Guinevere (gwin´ ə vēr) 🐾 In ARTHURIAN LEGEND, Guinevere was King Arthur's wife and queen. In the best-known story about her, Guinevere fell in love with the knight Sir Lancelot, which led to the downfall of Arthur and the end of Camelot.

The gallant knight Sir Lancelot saved Guinevere from death by fire and carried her away on his horse.

H

Hades (hād´ ēz) 🐚 In GREEK
MYTHOLOGY, Hades was the god of
the Underworld. The gods ZEUS and
POSEIDON were his brothers. Hades
lived in a palace and drove a black
chariot drawn by four black horses.
Hades became another name for the
Underworld. [*See also* PERSEPHONE,
HADES, AND DEMETER.]

Hainuwele (hī nü wē´ lē) 🐚
In Indonesian mythology, the goddess Hainuwele was born miraculous-
ly from a drop of blood. One day a man
named Ameta found a coconut, even
though no coconut palm trees yet
existed. That night when he slept,
Ameta dreamed that a man told him
to plant the coconut in the earth.
When he did so, the nut grew into a
tall palm tree in three days and then
blossomed. When Ameta tried to cut
the blossoms, he slashed his finger
and his blood fell on a leaf. Three days
later, Hainuwele had magically grown
on that spot. In another three days,
the child grew into a powerful deity.
She would later die in order to bring
great benefits to her people. [*See also*
DISMEMBERMENT; DYING GOD; GREAT GOD-
DESS; HAINUWELE, TRIALS OF; KUTOYIS.]

Hanuman (hä´ nü män) 🐚
The powerful and wily king of the
monkeys, Hanuman appears in INDIAN
MYTHOLOGY. He was the son of a
nymph (nature spirit) and the wind
god Pavana. In the Indian epic the
RAMAYANA, Hanuman uses his magic
skills to help RAMA rescue SITA when
she is kidnapped by the Rakshas. [*See
also* RAMA'S QUEST FOR SITA.]

Hawaiian Creation Myths
(hə wī´ yən) 🐚 The Hawaiian
story of CREATION is told in a poem
called the *Kumilipo*. As in many such
stories, the universe began in darkness. In the Hawaiian myth a series of
spirits formed, representing varying
degrees of darkness. Light appeared
very slowly.

The original darkness gave birth
to the first couple, the male Kumilipo,
meaning "essence of darkness," and
the female Po'ele, meaning "darkness
itself." They began giving birth to
living things, including seeds and
insects that hide in the darkness of
the earth and shellfish that live in the
dark depths of the sea. Kumilipo and
Po'ele were followed by several generations of parental pairs. Couples

Trials of Hainuwele (hī nü wē´ lē)

The goddess HAINUWELE of Indonesian myths was brought into being when a man's blood fell upon a coconut leaf. Three days later, Hainuwele had magically grown in that spot. In another three days, she was a powerful deity.

The people held a celebration and danced around Hainuwele as she produced gifts from her body for them. They held a rope and wrapped it around the goddess as they danced. However, some of the men pressed too close to Hainuwele. They crowded her until she could not move; they forced her into a pit and covered her with earth. Hainuwele cried for help, but no one paid any attention. They buried her alive.

The next morning, a man dug up the dead goddess. He chopped her body into pieces and buried most of them in different places. But he gave the arms to another goddess named Satene.

From the buried parts of Hainuwele's body, plants grew that people could eat. So Hainuwele's death, like that of CORN MOTHER in NATIVE NORTH AMERICAN MYTHOLOGY, provided a continuing source of food for her people. But Hainuwele's body also provided something more mysterious—the essence of humanity.

The goddess Satene made a doorway of Hainuwele's arms, and then she instructed the people to walk through the opening. Some were able to go through the doorway, and they remained human beings. Others, however, could not pass through the opening and they became animals or spirits. Then Satene left the people on their own and was never seen again.

In another version of the myth, the dead Hainuwele built a spiral, or LABYRINTH, through which people had to pass to see her. This gateway went to the Underworld. Those who could pass through it and visit Hainuwele could then return to life. [*See also* DISMEMBERMENT; FERTILITY MYTHS; GREAT GODDESS; REBIRTH AND RESURRECTION; SACRIFICE; UNDERWORLD, DESCENT TO.]

continued giving birth to creatures that lived and thrived by night. As yet, there were no human beings.

Little by little, light began to appear in the world. The wind and the dawn came into being. Spirits named Po-ne-e-aku and Poneie-mai were born, representing "night leaving" and "night pregnant." Finally two spirits of lesser darkness, Po-kinikini and Po-he'enalu, began giving birth to human beings. A woman called the Dark La'ila'a and a man called the Dark Ki'i were among the first creatures to see true daylight. [*See also* POLYNESIAN MYTHOLOGY.]

Hecate (hek´ ət) 🐚 A goddess of the Underworld in GREEK MYTHOLOGY, Hecate was a Titan—one of a number of deities who were overthrown by ZEUS and the Olympians. Hecate often used witchcraft, though she sometimes granted people good luck. She was also a goddess of crossroads—which were haunted places in many Greek stories. [*See also* UNDERWORLD, DESCENT TO.]

Helen (hel´ ən) 🐚 Helen was the daughter of ZEUS and a mortal woman named LEDA. The most beautiful woman in the world, Helen married Menelaus, the king of Sparta. But the Trojan prince Paris kidnapped her and took her to the city of Troy. The Greeks and Spartans fought the Trojans for ten years to get Helen back. The Greek poet Homer told of the Trojan War in the epic poem the *ILIAD*.

Hephaestus (he fes´ təs) 🐚 Hephaestus (or Hephaistos) was the Greek god of fire and the forge. He is known as Vulcan in ROMAN AND ETRUSCAN MYTHOLOGY. He was the son of HERA and possibly ZEUS, one of whom threw him out of heaven, crippling him for all eternity. Each of the CYCLOPES, a race of malicious one-eyed giants, served a turn working for Hephaestus.

The lame god Hephaestus was romantically involved with various goddesses. According to the *ODYSSEY*, he was married to the goddess of love

This painting shows Helen being kidnapped by Paris, the act that started the Trojan War.

herself, APHRODITE. She, however, fell in love with ARES, the god of war. The sun god Helios spotted the lovers together and told Hephaestus, who set a trap and caught them in an invisible net. Hephaestus summoned all the Olympian gods, who laughed at the guilty pair. Aphrodite fled to Cyprus in shame.

Hera (hâr´ ə) 🐚 In GREEK MYTHOLOGY, Hera was the queen of the gods. She was the daughter of the gods

Labors of Hercules (hėr´ kyə lēz)

The goddess HERA hated Hercules because he was the son of her husband ZEUS and a mortal woman. One time, Hera drove Hercules mad, and he unknowingly killed his wife and children. As penance (a voluntary self-punishment) for his misdeed, Hercules agreed to carry out a series of 12 labors.

For his first three labors, Hercules killed a terrible lion that could not be slain with weapons, slew a nine-headed monster called the Hydra, and captured a sacred stag. For his fourth labor, he chased and captured a ferocious boar. His fifth labor was to clean the filthy stables of King Augeas of Elis. Hercules killed a flock of man-eating birds for his sixth labor.

For his next three labors, Hercules captured a mad bull, captured man-eating horses, and took a girdle belonging to Hippolyta, the queen of the Amazons.

Hercules' last three labors were to capture a herd of oxen by killing their owner Geryon, a monster with three bodies, to steal the apples of the Hesperides, the daughters of Night, and to make a dangerous trip to the Underworld.

It took Hercules 12 years to finish the labors, but he was then freed of his guilt and made immortal. [*See also* REBIRTH AND RESURRECTION; TRIALS AND TESTS; UNDERWORLD, DESCENT TO.]

watched over childbirth and protected women. During the Trojan War, Hera supported the Greeks because she was angry with the Trojan prince Paris for choosing APHRODITE as the most beautiful goddess. The peacock was Hera's sacred bird. In ROMAN AND ETRUSCAN MYTHOLOGY, Hera was known as Juno. The month of June is named for her.

Hercules (hėr´ kyə lēz) 🐚 A

hero in GREEK MYTHOLOGY, Hercules was the son of ZEUS and Alcmena, a mortal woman. He was fantastically strong from the time of his birth. When he was an infant, the goddess HERA sent two serpents to kill him in his crib, but Hercules slew them both. The mighty hero was famous for the 12

CRONOS and Rhea and the mother of several gods. Hera once urged the other gods to conspire against her husband ZEUS, but the attempt failed. As the goddess of marriage, Hera

After his death, Hercules acended to Mount Olympus on a horse-drawn chariot.

labors he insisted on doing after he unknowingly committed a terrible crime. [*See also* ALCESTIS; GREEK CREATION MYTHS; LABORS OF HERCULES; REBIRTH AND RESURRECTION; TRIALS AND TESTS; UNDERWORLD, DESCENT TO.]

Hermes (hėr´mēz) ● In

GREEK MYTHOLOGY, Hermes was the son of ZEUS and Maia, the daughter of the Titan Atlas. Hermes was the swift messenger of the gods and had wings on both his hat and sandals. He carried a magic staff entwined with snakes called a caduceus. Hermes was known as Mercury in ROMAN AND ETRUSCAN MYTHOLOGY.

The ancient Greek sculptor Praxiteles made many statues, including this one of Hermes holding the young god Dionysus.

Hermes was a TRICKSTER, clever at stealing objects from the other gods, including a bow belonging to APOLLO, the girdle of APHRODITE, the trident (three-pronged spear) of POSEIDON, and the tools of HEPHAESTUS. He once stole a herd of cows from Apollo and hid their tracks. Hermes was found out only because he was caught using cow-gut strings on the lyre he had just invented. But Hermes talked Apollo into taking the lyre in payment.

Hero and Heroine ● In

myths from around the world, male heroes and female heroines used their courage, strength, and intelligence to overcome great obstacles. Their stories were told around campfires for thousands of years. Long poems called epics were composed to celebrate their accomplishments. Heroic epics such as *GILGAMESH* and *BEOWULF* provided some of our earliest written stories.

Some champions, such as CUCHULAIN, Finn, HERCULES, MWINDO, and VAINAMOINEN showed unusual abilities from childhood. They possessed extraordinary strength, magic powers, special weapons, or supernatural friends and protectors. Their parentage was usually mysterious or supernatural, sometimes resulting from a miraculous birth. Some heroes, such as WATERJAR BOY, had to search for and discover their father. Most had to undergo TRIALS AND TESTS to

Hopi Emergence (hō´ pē)

Some CREATION stories in NATIVE NORTH AMERI-CAN MYTHOLOGY tell how animals and people emerged (came out) onto the earth from another place. According to the Hopi Indians, the gods TAWA and SPIDER WOMAN first lived in the Underworld. Together they created the other gods. By singing, they created the earth.

Tawa created pictures in his mind and Spider Woman made them out of clay. These were animals, and the two gods brought them to life with magic. Then the gods created beings much like themselves. These were people, and the gods sang them to life. Then Tawa, the sun god, went to live in the sky. From there he lighted and warmed the earth below.

Spider Woman decided to take the people and animals out of the Underworld onto the earth. First, she separated the people into tribes and gave each tribe a name. Then Spider Woman led them all upward, through a small opening called a *sipapu*. The people and animals spread out over the newly created earth and went on with their lives.

The Hopi build special rooms for religious and social use called kivas. Often round and underground, the kivas always have a small *sipapu* in the floor for the gods to come through. According to Hopi stories, we now live in the fourth world. After an APOCALYPSE good people will be reborn, emerging into a better fifth world. [*See also* ACOMA CREATION MYTH; APACHE CREATION MYTHS; BRAHMA; DJANGGAWUL DREAMING CREATION; KIOWA CREATION MYTHS; NAVAJO EMERGENCE; REBIRTH AND RESURRECTION; ZUNI CREATION MYTHS.]

prove their worth. Some, like GAWAIN and SITA, were models of perfection. Others, like Lemminkainen, provided examples of how not to behave.

A hero or heroine would often go on a QUEST for something of value, such as knowledge, wealth, fame, eternal life, or spiritual growth. The JOURNEY QUESTS of Gilgamesh, ISIS, JASON, and RAMA took them to strange places, even to the Underworld. Some heroes, such as ODYSSEUS, used cleverness as much as courage to complete their journeys.

Many heroes and some heroines, including ACHILLES and BRYNHILD, were warriors. Others such as KUTOYIS; LITUOLONE; PERSEUS; SIEGFRIED; and THESEUS became famous for MONSTER SLAYING. Some were not fighters at all, but offered themselves as a SACRIFICE for their people. Those who brought civilization to a people, like QUETZALCOATL and OSIRIS, were called "cultural heroes." Even many sly and apparently unheroic TRICKSTERS were cultural heroes.

Although a champion was usually successful, his or her own life might be lost in the process. After everything they went through, some heroes and heroines reached a peak of self-understanding called apotheosis. [*See also AENEID;* ARTHURIAN LEGEND; *COOLEY, CATTLE RAID OF;* EDDAS; *ENUMA ELISH;* FATHER, SEARCH FOR; FINN AND THE FIANNA; GRAIL QUEST; *ILIAD; KALEVALA; LEABHAR GABHALA;* LEMMINKAINEN'S DEATH AND RESURRECTION; *MABINOGION; MAHABHARATA;* MANU AND THE FISH; *NIBELUN-*

The god Horus is often represented as a falcon.

GENLIED; NIHONGI; ODYSSEY; POPUL VUH; RAMAYANA; RIG VEDA; UNDERWORLD, DESCENT TO.]

Hittite Mythology (hi′ tīt′)

The myths of the ancient Hittite people included a PANTHEON of thousands of deities. The Hittite kingdom (established about 1750 B.C. and destroyed about 1200 B.C.) extended from the Bosporus and the Aegean coast across much of what is now Turkey. Some scholars believe that Hittite songs and myths influenced the *THEOGONY*, a work written by the Greek poet Hesiod (c. 800 B.C.).

Hyacinthus and Apollo
(hī ə sin′ thus) (ə päl′ ō)

The Spartan prince Hyacinthus was a favorite of the god APOLLO. One day, when Apollo was teaching Hyacinthus how to throw the discus, they had a competition to see who could cast it farther. Apollo's discus accidentally struck Hyacinthus in the forehead, killing him. Apollo was heartbroken over his friend's death and wept for him. Wherever Hyacinthus' blood hit the ground, beautiful blue flowers sprang up. They were called hyacinths after the slain prince.

According to most stories, the West Wind was really the cause of Hyacinthus' death. The wind was infatuated with Hyacinth and grew furiously jealous of Apollo's attentions to the beautiful prince. The West Wind deliberately blew the discus off course and aimed it at Hyacinthus' head. [*See also* NARCISSUS, DEATH OF.]

Horus (hôr′ us)
Two deities in EGYPTIAN MYTHOLOGY were named Horus. The first was a sun god, the brother of OSIRIS, ISIS, and SETH. The other was the son of Osiris and Isis. In some stories, the two gods merged into one.

Hyacinthus (hī ə sin′ thus)
In GREEK MYTHOLOGY, Hyacinthus was a beautiful prince from the city-state of Sparta. He was loved by many people and gods because of his beauty. [*See also* HYACINTHUS AND APOLLO.]

I J

Iliad (il´ ē əd) ☙ The *Iliad* is an epic poem about the Trojan War. It is said to have been written by a Greek poet named Homer in about 900 or 850 B.C. An actual Trojan War took place about 1230 B.C. It was probably fought over trade routes, although the war of legend was fought over HELEN, the most beautiful woman in the world.

Helen, who was the wife of the Spartan king Menelaus, was kidnapped by the Trojan prince Paris. A huge Greek army besieged Troy, trying to get Helen back. The fighting went on for ten years, with neither side victorious. Then the Greek general Agamemnon kidnapped a priest's daughter, Chryseis, to be his mistress. For that insult to the gods, APOLLO sent a plague against the Greeks. Agamemnon agreed to give up Chryseis only if he could have a woman named Briseis instead. Briseis was the mistress of the Greek warrior ACHILLES, who did surrender her to Agamemnon. But Achilles then angrily refused to fight any more.

Achilles was the greatest warrior alive, and his absence from the battlefield was a disaster to the Greeks. Even when Agamemnon apologized and offered to return Briseis, Achilles stayed in his tent. Finally, Achilles' friend Patroclos insisted on fighting in the reluctant hero's place. Patroclos put on Achilles' armor and wreaked havoc upon the Trojans until he was killed by Prince Hector.

The death of his friend brought Achilles back to the battlefield. Achilles killed Hector and, still enraged, refused to return the prince's body to his family. King Priam, Hector's elderly father, crossed the battle line with gifts for Achilles. Moved by the old man's pleas, Achilles finally gave up Hector's body.

The *Iliad* ends with Hector's funeral. But the poem makes clear that Achilles would soon be killed in battle and that Troy would fall to the Greeks. [*See also* GREEK MYTHOLOGY.]

Inanna-Ishtar (ē nän´ ä, ish´ tär) ☙ In ancient SUMERIAN MYTHOLOGY, Inanna was called the Queen of Heaven and Earth. Also a warrior goddess, Inanna represented good in the eternal battle between good and evil. Her older sister Ereshkigal, the goddess of the Underworld, was sometimes interpreted as being Inanna's darker half.

Inanna and the Underworld
(ē nän´ ä)

According to the stories of ancient SUMERIAN MYTHOLOGY, the goddess Inanna went to the land of the dead to achieve wisdom. The Underworld deity, Ereshkigal, was Inanna's sister and also her bitter enemy. Ereshkigal allowed Inanna to pass through the seven gates of her kingdom, but then Ereshkigal had her sister stripped naked and brought before judges. They put Inanna to death.

Inanna's friend and servant Ninshubur appealed to several gods to come to Inanna's aid. Only one agreed to help—Inanna's grandfather ENKI, the god of wisdom. He created two sexless creatures named Kur-gar-ra and Gala-tur-ra and sent them to the Underworld. Acting on Enki's instructions, Kur-gar-ra and Gala-tur-ra sprinkled Inanna's corpse with the "food of life" and the "water of life." Inanna came to life again and returned to the world of the living. But somebody had to take Inanna's place among the dead, and Inanna felt that her inattentive husband Dumuzi would be a good choice.

In some stories, Dumuzi went down to the Underworld and was, in turn, saved by his sister, Geshtinanna. She agreed to spend half of each year in the Underworld, allowing Dumuzi to return to the world of the living during that time. His yearly stay in the land of the dead made Dumuzi a more caring, thoughtful husband, and her husband's absences made Inanna a more appreciative wife. For half of every year, they lived and ruled together happily. In other versions of the myth, Dumuzi was called TAMMUZ, and Innana herself rescued him. [*See also* INANNA-ISHTAR; PERSEPHONE, HADES, AND DEMETER; REBIRTH AND RESURRECTION; TRIALS AND TESTS; UNDERWORLD, DESCENT TO.]

Inanna is sometimes portrayed with snakes, as in this sculpture.

In BABYLONIAN MYTHOLOGY, the same goddess was called Ishtar. In some stories she was a goddess of love or healing; in others, she was a goddess of war. Ishtar was often depicted carrying weapons and accompanied by a lion. [*See also* ENKI; GREAT GODDESS; INANNA AND THE UNDERWORLD; TAMMUZ.]

Indian Mythology ✏ Stories
about a CREATION, gods and goddesses, and HEROES AND HEROINES were written down as long as 3,000 years ago in India. They were recorded in works named the *RIG VEDA*, the *MAHABHARATA*, and the *RAMAYANA*. A complex and changing PANTHEON of gods worked together in Indian myths. For example, according to the early stories, the warrior INDRA made creation possible

Incan Flood (inˊ kən)

Stories of a great FLOOD were told by the Inca of South America. According to one myth, a SHAMAN named Sommay had twin sons. The firstborn, Tamendonare, was a good husband and father. However, the secondborn, Ariconte, was a constant source of trouble. He fought with his neighbors and did as many bad deeds as his brother Tamendonare did good ones.

In one fight, Ariconte tore the arm off his enemy. Grasping the still-bleeding arm, he stormed to his brother's house. Ariconte screamed that his brother was a coward who could not even defend his wife and children.

Tamendonare replied that if Ariconte was really so brave, he would have brought the whole body of his enemy. In fury, Ariconte threw the arm at his brother's door. Magically, the rest of the people of that village disappeared. They had been taken up to heaven by the gods, leaving only the twin brothers and their families on earth.

Tamendonare looked around in amazement. He stamped the ground so furiously that a huge fountain sprang up. The water gushed all the way to the clouds, then fell back onto the earth. As the waters covered the land, the brothers and their families scrambled up the highest mountain and clung to trees. After a time, Ariconte's wife threw down a piece of fruit. When they heard it splash, they knew the water was still high.

When the floodwaters finally went down, the two brothers and their wives discovered that they were the only people left on earth. They became the ancestors of two different tribes that never stopped quarreling.

NATIVE CENTRAL AND SOUTH AMERICAN MYTHOLOGY also includes another flood story in which a sorcerer broke so many calabashes (gourds) of water that he flooded the earth. [*See also* APACHE CREATION MYTHS; APOCALYPSE; FARO; MANABOZHO; MANU AND THE FISH; MAYAN CREATION MYTHS; MOUNTAIN; NAVAJO EMERGENCE; PROMETHEUS, DEEDS OF; RUDRA DESTROYS THE WORLD; STAR WOMAN AND THE TWINS; SUMERIAN/BABYLONIAN FLOOD.]

when he killed a dragon that had swallowed all the PRIMAL WATERS. Then the gods Varuna and Mitra presided over the new universe. The indestructible giant TREE, Asvattha, represented the Indian cosmos.

BRAHMA was the creator god of later Indian myths, but VISNU and SIVA influenced human activities. Visnu was best known through his avatars KRISHNA and RAMA. An avatar was the embodiment of a god in human form and was therefore both a deity and a human hero. [*See also* DANU; DRAUPADI; DURGA; GANESA; GANGES, BIRTH OF THE; HANUMAN; KALI; MANU; MAYA; PANDAVAS; PARVATI; RUDRA DESTROYS THE WORLD; SITA.]

Indra (in´ drə) ☙ In INDIAN MYTHOLOGY, Indra was a god of the sky, fertility, and war. With a thunderbolt, he killed a monster that kept water from the land. Indra built a great palace but became humble when he learned that the ants in his doorway had been Indras in previous lives. [*See also* DANU; FERTILITY MYTHS; MONSTER SLAYING; RIG VEDA CREATION.]

Io (ī´ ō) ☙ In GREEK MYTHOLOGY Io was a priestess of the goddess HERA.

Isis (ī´ səs) ☙ The Egyptian Mother Goddess, Isis was the granddaughter of the sun god RA. She tricked Ra into telling her his secret name, which gave

This bronze statue of the god Indra was made in the 1100s or 1200s.

her great power. Isis was the wife and sister of OSIRIS, and HORUS was their son. [*See also* EGYPTIAN MYTHOLOGY; GREAT GODDESS; OSIRIS; SETH.]

Izanami and Izanagi (its ə nä´ mē) (its ə nä´ gē) ☙ In JAPANESE MYTHOLOGY the youngest gods in the heavens were a brother and sister named Izanami and Izanagi. Together they created the islands of Japan, as well as gods for everything in the earth, sea, and sky. [*See also* AMATERASU; JAPANESE CREATION MYTHS.]

Japanese Mythology ☙

Based on very old stories, Japanese myths are told with many variations. The earliest are from the traditions of Shinto, an ancient Japanese religion that believed everything in nature has a spirit or god. Therefore, when the gods IZANAMI AND IZANAGI gave birth to the forests, mountains, streams, waterfalls, wind, and elements of the earth, they also created gods for each of them.

In the sixth century A.D., additional myths and deities were introduced into Japan through the Buddhist religion. Many Japanese stories and characters draw on both Shinto and Buddhist traditions. In the eighth century A.D. the myths were written down in the *Kojiki* and the *NIHONGI*. [*See also* AMATERASU; JAPANESE CREATION MYTHS.]

Jason (jās´ ən) ☙ In GREEK MYTHOLOGY Jason was the bold leader of

Japanese Creation Myths

According to JAPANESE MYTHOLOGY the world was created by a god and goddess working together. When the universe separated into heaven and earth, the earth was all under water. A reed plant sprouted and became the first god. A whole family of gods followed. The youngest were a brother and sister named IZANAMI AND IZANAGI.

Izanami and Izanagi stood together on a rainbow, which was called the Floating Bridge of Heaven. In some stories, Izanagi thrust the Jewel Spear of Heaven into the waters below. When he drew it out, the drops from the tip formed islands. In other stories, the two young gods were given the job of organizing islands that already existed.

On these islands of Japan, Izanami and Izanagi built a palace. They performed a marriage ceremony, but Izanami made a mistake. When she met her new husband, she spoke first. Because of this, they had to do the ceremony over again.

The newly married couple created everything in nature. Their most beautiful daughter, AMATERASU, became the goddess of the sun. Her bad-tempered brother, Susa-no-wo, became the storm god.

When Izanami died giving birth to the fire god, Kagu-Tsuchi, she went to Yomi, the land of death. Izanagi followed her there, but it was too late to bring her back. In fact, Izanagi had to outwit and battle terrible monsters to save his own life and return to the surface of the earth.

After his escape from the land of death, Izanagi washed in the sea. That action created many gods, including those of the ocean. In some stories, the gods of the sun, moon, and underworld came from Izanagi washing his eyes and nose. [*See also* CREATION; GREAT GODDESS; MONSTER SLAYING; "ORPHEUS" THEME; UNDERWORLD, DESCENT TO; WORLD PARENTS.]

the Argonauts, warrior heroes who had many adventures on their QUEST for the legendary Golden Fleece. [*See also* JASON AND THE GOLDEN FLEECE; MEDEA.]

Journey Quest (jər´ nē kwest´)

🍄 In myths from around the world, the QUEST of a hero or heroine often involved a long, difficult journey. Gilgamesh, a hero of the oldest stories in BABYLONIAN MYTHOLOGY, traveled far and wide in search of eternal life. In

An ancient fresco, or wall painting, from the city of Pompeii shows Jason standing below his uncle Pelias.

Jason and the Golden Fleece (jās´ ən)

In GREEK MYTHOLOGY, the hero Jason was the heir to the throne of Thessaly, a region of Greece. When his uncle Pelias took the throne, Jason's mother sent him to be raised by the centaur Chiron, who was half man and half horse.

On his way back to Thessaly, Jason lost one sandal while helping an old woman cross a stream. Meanwhile, Pelias had been warned by a prophet to beware of a visitor with one sandal. So—hoping that Jason would be killed in the attempt—Pelias challenged him to make a dangerous journey to get the golden fleece of a sacred ram.

Jason collected warriors to go with him on a ship called the *Argo*. The goddess HERA was fond of Jason. So he and his warriors—called the Argonauts—had good winds and good luck on their trip to Colchis, the land of the golden fleece. During their voyage, the Argonauts killed harpies (winged monsters) that were torturing an old prophet. They also visited the Amazons, a race of women warriors, and saw PROMETHEUS chained to his rock.

When the Argonauts reached Colchis, its king, Aeetis, thought up new challenges to prevent Jason from taking the fleece. So Hera persuaded APHRODITE, the goddess of love, to make the king's daughter MEDEA fall in love with Jason. Medea was a beautiful and powerful witch. Relying on her advice, Jason plowed a field with two fire-breathing bulls. He planted the teeth of a DRAGON and defeated fierce warriors that sprouted from the teeth. Jason then stole the fleece and fled Colchis, taking Medea with him. Medea killed her own brother when he chased them and saved the Argonauts from a giant.

After a tricky passage through the Wandering Rocks and past the Sirens, who tried to lure them to destruction, the Argonauts reached Thessaly. There, Medea arranged the murder of King Pelias. In spite of Medea's help, Jason later abandoned her. [*See also* JOURNEY QUEST.]

GREEK MYTHOLOGY, JASON and his followers made a perilous journey to the land of Colchis in search of the Golden Fleece. In CELTIC MYTHOLOGY the goddess RHIANNON went to the Underworld to rescue her son, Pryderi. And in POLYNESIAN MYTHOLOGY the goddess PELE traveled widely in search of her husband. [*See also* AENEAS; AUSTRALIAN ABORIGINAL MYTHOLOGY; DREAMING; *GILGAMESH;* GRAIL QUEST; HERO AND HEROINE; NAVAJO TWINS; "ORPHEUS" THEME; PERSEUS; TRIALS AND TESTS; UNDERWORLD, DESCENT TO; WANJIRU; WATERJAR BOY.]

Juno (ju´ nō) ☙ *See* HERA.

Jupiter (jū´ pi tėr) ☙ *See* ZEUS.

Kachinas

Kachinas (kä chē´ nəz) 🐚 In the myths of the Hopi Indians and other Pueblo groups in the American Southwest, kachinas were ancestor spirits and NATURE SPIRITS. They lived in the San Francisco Peaks of present-day Arizona and in other locations associated with water. Hopi religious activities still feature dancers dressed as kachinas. Kachina dolls are given to children and also play an important role in religious rites. [*See also* NATIVE NORTH AMERICAN MYTHOLOGY.]

This Hopi cloth shows figures and symbols that represent Kachinas.

Kalevala (kä lə vä´ lä) 🐚 Stories based on the traditional songs of Finland were collected in a work called the *Kalevala*, which was first published in the mid-1800s. The name *Kalevala* refers to the Kaleva District, a mythical land where the stories take place. [*See also* FINNIC CREATION MYTHS; FINNIC MYTHOLOGY; LEMMINKAINEN'S DEATH AND RESURRECTION; VAINAMOINEN.]

Kali (kä´ lē) 🐚 One of the fiercest forms taken by the great goddess Devi of INDIAN MYTHOLOGY, Kali had black skin, four arms, and sharp teeth. She wore a necklace of skulls (or sometimes a cobra). Kali could be both creative and destructive, and in Indian myths both aspects of the goddess were considered important. Although Kali was sometimes pictured with a right hand raised in blessing, a left hand always held a bloody sword. Her partner was the god SIVA.

In one of her most famous adventures, Kali fought against a terrible demon named Raktavija. Unable to destroy the monster with her weapons, she killed him by drinking all his blood. [*See also* DURGA; GREAT

GODDESS; *MAHABHARATA;* MONSTERS AND MYTHICAL BEASTS; MONSTER SLAYING; PARVATI; *RAMAYANA;* *RIG VEDA.*]

Krishna (krish´nə) 🐚 An avatar—or embodiment in human form—of the god VISNU in INDIAN MYTHOLOGY, Krishna had many characteristics of a TRICKSTER. As a child he stole butter from his mother, but he usually charmed his way out of trouble. He was, however, also a child-hero who killed a vicious female demon.

Portrayed with blue skin, Krishna is seated here next to a woman.

Kiowa Creation Myths
(kī´ə wə)

According to their CREATION story, the Kiowa Indians were once a very large tribe, and they lived within the earth. As in EMERGENCE stories from the NATIVE NORTH AMERICAN MYTHOLOGY of other groups, the time came when the people wanted to move to the earth's surface. They found a hollow log that connected the two worlds. Like children being born from the Mother Earth, they crawled through the log one by one. Only a few of them had gotten out when a pregnant woman got stuck in the log. Then no others could pass and many had to remain in the Underworld. That is why the Kiowa tribe on earth is not very large.

Those who made it through the log were glad to be in the outside world. They called themselves Kwuda, which means "coming out." They began hunting, and some of the tribe split off and went away because of an argument over an antelope. No one knows what became of them, but the main Kiowa tribe soon learned how to live on the land. [*See also* ACOMA CREATION MYTH; APACHE CREATION MYTHS; HOPI EMERGENCE; NAVAJO EMERGENCE.]

As an adult prince, Krishna was depicted as a blue-skinned god of love, playing a flute. He represented both human strengths and human failings. Krishna's music calmed storms, quieted rivers, and caused

Kuan Yin and the Underworld
(kwän´ yin´)

In CHINESE MYTHOLOGY KUAN YIN was a gentle Mother Goddess and the goddess of mercy. She protected women and children, and women who wanted to become pregnant prayed to her.

In the oldest myths about Kuan Yin, the deity was male. But sometime between A.D. 600 and 1100, the character was changed to a female. Kuan Yin was able to take many forms, and in JAPANESE MYTHOLOGY she appeared as a many-armed male deity named Kwannon.

In other versions of the myth, Kuan Yin was originally a mortal princess, the daughter of a cruel father. She was expected to marry, but she wanted to devote herself to a temple instead. In some stories, she strangled herself rather than marry. In others, her father continued to torment her. He first made sure that the women of the temple treated Kuan Yin badly. However, friendly animals helped her do the seemingly impossible chores assigned to her. Furious, her father set the temple on fire. Kuan Yin put out the fire with her hands, proving that she had divine power. Nevertheless, her father was still determined to kill her, and he finally had a servant strangle her.

After her death, Kuan Yin was taken to the Underworld on the back of a tiger. At first she was terrified, but she overcame her fear and began to sing. Her voice was so beautiful that it relieved the suffering of those who lived in the land of the dead. The soothing sounds made the king of the Underworld unhappy, so he sent Kuan Yin away. She returned to earth and went to live on an island. From there, she continued to comfort the living and the dead. [*See also* UNDERWORLD, DESCENT TO.]

maidens to fall in love with him. [*See ALSO* DRAUPADI; *MAHABHARATA;* PANDAVAS; *RAMAYANA.*]

Kuan Yin (kwän´ yin´) 🐦 The Mother Goddess in CHINESE MYTHOLOGY, Kuan Yin represented protection and was associated with fertility. Kuan Yin was male in some of the oldest myths, but the character was female in later stories. Her name Kuan means "the earth." Yin stands for "the feminine power" that, according to Buddhist tradition, balances the male power called yang. [*See also* FERTILITY MYTHS; GREAT GODDESS; KUAN YIN AND THE UNDERWORLD.]

This early wooden statue is of the Chinese mother goddess Kuan Yin.

Adventures of Kutoyis (kṳ tō´ yēs)

In NATIVE NORTH AMERICAN MYTHOLOGY of the Blackfoot Indians, Kutoyis was a hero who battled various monsters. He was brought to life by an old man and woman whose two daughters had both married the same warrior. The old couple had thought this fine son-in-law would take care of them as they grew older. However, the warrior grew selfish and refused to take care of his in-laws, so they sought help elsewhere.

One day, the old man picked up a clot of blood from a wounded buffalo. He hid the blood, took it back to his lodge, and told his wife to put it into the water that was boiling over the fire. When she did so, they heard screams. The old couple hastened to remove the magical baby boy who had grown there.

They named the child Kutoyis, which meant "clot of blood." They knew their son-in-law would not let them raise a boy, so they said it was a girl. When the child was only four days old, he insisted they tie him between the lodge poles. They did, and Kutoyis grew instantly into a full-size young man. He shot and killed the warrior with his arrows, then killed the daughters who had allowed their parents to be treated so badly.

Next Kutoyis set out to make things right in the rest of the world. He killed any monsters, human or animal, who did not take good care of the elders of their community. He saved a group of people from the Wind Sucker monster who had swallowed them. Kutoyis allowed himself to be sucked in, and killed that creature from inside.

The worst monster of all was Man Eater. Knowing that this monster would kill, cook, and eat him, Kutoyis planned ahead. He asked a young girl to take his bones, throw them to the dogs, and call his name. When she did so, Kutoyis rose from the pile of bones and returned to Man Eater's lodge. After he had been killed, eaten, and resurrected four times, Kutoyis killed Man Eater and his family, ridding the world of evil. [*See also* HAINUWELE; LITUOLONE; MONSTER SLAYING; NAVAJO TWINS; REBIRTH AND RESURRECTION.]

Kutoyis (kṳ tō´ yēs) ☙ In the stories of the Blackfoot and in other NATIVE NORTH AMERICAN MYTHOLOGY, Kutoyis was a supernatural hero. His story included a miraculous birth from a clot of blood, TRIALS AND TESTS, MONSTER SLAYING, and death and resurrection. He was a protector of his people, especially the elders. [*See also* KUTOYIS, ADVENTURES OF.]

Labyrinth (lab´ə rinth) 🐚 A type of maze, a labyrinth often represents a difficult journey in myths. When a hero or heroine finds the way through a labyrinth, faces whatever is there, and escapes, the story represents REBIRTH AND RESURRECTION.

In GREEK MYTHOLOGY, the master craftsman Daedalus designed a labyrinth for King Minos of Crete. Daedalus and his son Icarus later sought to escape the labyrinth on artificial wings. Daedalus soared to freedom, but Icarus crashed to his death in the sea. The Greek hero THESEUS later found his way through the same labyrinth and killed the Minotaur, a half-human, half-bull monster that lived there. [*See also* MONSTER SLAYING.]

Leabhar Gabhala (lür gä´ vä lä) 🐚 *The Book of the Taking of Ireland*, or *Leabhar Gabhala*, is an important source of CELTIC MYTHOLOGY. It includes stories about the goddess DANU, the god Midir, and other supernatural beings. Those deities were believed to have lived in Ireland before a series of invasions by the ancient European people known as the Celts. Both the ancient gods and the human invaders are considered ancestors of the current inhabitants of Ireland. The later stories collected in the *Leabhar Gabhala* blend Celtic myths with biblical accounts of the CREATION, ADAM and EVE, and Noah. [*See also* MIDIR AND ETAIN.]

Leda (lēd´ ə) 🐚 *See* LEDA AND THE SWAN.

Legba (ləg´ ba) 🐚 In the mythology of West Africa, Legba was a TRICKSTER god. He often appeared as an old man dressed in rags, carrying a walking stick. He was the god of entrances and crossroads. The son of the high deity MAWU, Legba knew all languages. When Mawu grew annoyed with Legba's pranks and withdrew from the earth to the heavens, the trickster became the messenger between gods and humans.

Legba was known as Eshu to the Yoruba of West Africa. Under

After her death, Leda was sometimes referred to as Nemesis.

Leda and the Swan (lēd´ə)

In GREEK MYTHOLOGY, Leda was the wife of Tyndarus, the king of Sparta. She bore Tyndarus at least one child—a daughter named Clytemnestra. But she also bore one or more offspring to ZEUS, the chief Olympian god.

As he often did with mortal women, Zeus fell in love with Leda from afar. As also was his habit, he disguised himself in order to seduce her. This time, he took the form of a beautiful swan. The union of Leda and Zeus produced an egg. The number of children that hatched from it varies from story to story. According to some versions of the myth, the egg contained the famous twin brothers Castor and Pollux. Other versions say that Pollux was Zeus' child, while Castor was the mortal son of Tyndarus. A beautiful girl named HELEN was also born from the egg.

All of Leda's offspring, whether mortal or otherwise, gained great fame. Clytemnestra married Agamemnon, the king of Argos, whom she eventually killed. The brothers Castor and Pollux were adventurers who traveled with JASON on his QUEST for the Golden Fleece. The twins proved inseparable even in death. Helen's beauty eventually caused the Trojan War. [See also ILIAD; JASON AND THE GOLDEN FLEECE.]

variations of both names, the trickster's stories eventually spread into South America, Cuba, Haiti, and the southern United States. [See also CARIBBEAN MYTHOLOGY.]

Lilith (lil´oth) 🐾 In Jewish, Christian, and Islamic mythology, Lilith was the first wife of ADAM. According to some stories, she claimed equality with Adam because they were created at the same time. She was expelled from paradise because she refused to serve her husband. Then God created EVE to be Adam's wife.

Lilith is usually described as a female demon. In Islamic stories, she was the wife of the devil and mother of all demons. In Jewish stories, Lilith was the first woman. But she left Eden, mated with demons, and then returned as the serpent that tempted Eve. [See also MONSTERS AND MYTHICAL BEASTS.]

Lemminkainen's Death and Resurrection (lem in kä ē´ nen)

In FINNIC MYTHOLOGY, Lemminkainen was a handsome young adventurer who was fond of both war and women. Although he was intelligent, his pride and recklessness often got him into trouble. His story was told in traditional Finnish songs that were collected into an epic called the KALEVALA.

Lemminkainen decided to go to North Farm (Northern Finland or Lapland) to find a wife. In some versions of the myth, he was interested in a certain maiden; in others he was just looking for an appropriate woman. His mother begged him not to go, insisting that he would surely die there. However, Lemminkainen could not be discouraged.

Either during the voyage or after he arrived, Lemminkainen was killed and his body cut into pieces. According to some stories, he hurried to North Farm and asked Louhi, the mistress of the house, for her daughter. Louhi, who was both a gracious hostess and a skillful witch, declared that Lemminkainen must first do several dangerous deeds. Lemminkainen attacked the tasks with his usual recklessness and was killed trying to carry them out. His body was thrown into the river of Death, and the son of Death cut it up.

Lemminkainen's mother carefully collected all of the pieces of her son's body. It took all of her magic to put them back together and bring him back to life. Lemminkainen lived through many more adventures, some in the company of the Finnish hero-brothers Vainamoinen and Ilmarinen. Unfortunately Lemminkainen grew no wiser. [*See also* DISMEMBERMENT; OSIRIS.]

Lituolone (lē tü lō´ nā)

In AFRICAN MYTHOLOGY, the Bantu hero Lituolone saved the human race. The Bantu were tormented by a monster named Kammapa, who ate everyone except one old woman. Without the help of a man, the old woman gave birth to Lituolone, who immediately grew to full size. Kammapa swallowed Lituolone, but the hero tore the monster apart from inside, releasing thousands of people. [*See also* HERO AND HEROINE; KUTOYIS; MONSTER SLAYING.]

Loki (lō´ kē)

In NORSE MYTHOLOGY, Loki was an evil god, a TRICKSTER who constantly caused trouble. Loki could change shape at will. His offspring were the wolf Fenrir; the eight-legged horse Sleipnir; Hel, the ruler of the dead; and the Midgard serpent. Loki played an important role in the death of the god BALDER. [*See also* BALDER, DEATH OF; RAGNAROK, END OF THE WORLD.]

Lone Man

In the myths told by the Mandan Indians, Lone Man was a creator spirit who helped to make the earth. He then spent much of his life in human form in order to teach people how to live. In some versions of the stories, he was called Only Man. [*See also* LONE MAN AND THE MANDAN CREATION; NATIVE NORTH AMERICAN MYTHOLOGY.]

Loki's Tricks (lō′ kē)

The god LOKI committed countless acts of mischief, with some being destructive.

The Norse gods lived in Asgard, in the heavens. The walls of Asgard once fell into disrepair. A stranger came and offered to rebuild them. In payment, he wanted the goddess FREYA.

Loki proposed that the gods accept this offer, but insisted that the stranger complete the job in six months. Loki would make sure that the stranger failed to meet this deadline, and the gods would not have to surrender Freya.

With the help of a stallion, the stranger made better time than Loki expected. So Loki turned himself into a mare, distracting the stallion and causing the stranger to fall behind schedule.

Loki took the forms of many other creatures. Sometimes his shape-shifting got him into trouble. As a hawk, he was captured by the giant Geirrod and locked in a box. Once, while being pursued by angry gods, Loki turned himself into a salmon to escape. But the gods caught him in a magic net and placed him in a cave, with a venomous serpent above him.

According to legend, Loki's wife Sigyn still stands before him in the cave, catching the serpent's venom in a bowl to keep it from falling on her husband. Every time she empties the bowl, a few drops fall on Loki's face and he shudders in agony, causing earthquakes. Loki will remain there until RAGNAROK, END OF THE WORLD.

Lone Man and the Mandan Creation

In the NATIVE NORTH AMERICAN MYTHOLOGY of the Mandan Indians, the world was dark at first and covered with PRIMAL WATERS. LONE MAN and a deity called First Creator walked along on the water. When they met a duck, they asked her how she could live on such a world. The duck dove deep beneath the water and brought them a bit of mud. She said food grew there.

As in other EARTH DIVER stories, the creator spirits expanded the mud into all the land. They also used it to make animals, humans, and plant life. Then Lone Man and First Creator went their separate ways to create the features of the earth. Heading north, Lone Man made the flat lands, water, and animals on that side of the river we now call the Missouri. On the south side of the river, First Creator made mountains, forests, streams, and animals.

The human beings that the two had created began to populate the earth. Then Lone Man had himself born in human form, and he taught the Mandans many skills for their survival and comfort. He also taught them religious ceremonies that would protect them from evil.

M

Mabinogion (ma bi nō´ jē ən)

🐚 Published in the 1800s, the *Mabinogion* contains 11 Welsh myths translated into English. These stories from CELTIC MYTHOLOGY were first written down in the Middle Ages, but they were based on much earlier Welsh and Irish oral narratives.

The *Mabinogion* is divided into three sections. *The Four Branches of the Mabinogi* consists of stories about RHIANNON, her son Pyderi, and other supernatural beings. *Independent Native Tales* includes "Kilhwch and Olwen," a story in which King Arthur appears. The third section of the *Mabinogion* deals with ARTHURIAN LEGEND and includes an early story about the knight Perceval.

Mahabharata (mä hä bä´ rä tä)

🐚 Hindu myths about many heroes and heroines and gods and goddesses are told in a long series of poems called the *Mahabharata*. The poems were written between 200 B.C. and A.D. 200 and compiled about A.D. 400. The 18 books of the *Mahabharata* make up the longest literary work in the world, a vast collection of Hindu thought and legend. In the section called the *Bhagavad Gita*, the god KRISHNA teaches the Pandava brother Arjuna how people should live and relate to their gods. The *Mahabharata* was written by a poet named Vyasa, who is also a character in the stories. [*See also* DRAUPADI; DURGA; GANESA; HERO AND HEROINE; INDIAN MYTHOLOGY; KALI; PANDAVAS; VISNU.]

Manabozho (mä nä bō´ zō)

🐚 In the myths of the Algonquin Indians, Manabozho was a powerful TRICKSTER spirit. Creator of the world and founder of sacred rituals, he often appeared as a human but could take any form. In some stories he was identified as the Great Hare. Like other Algonquin tricksters such as GLOOSCAP, Manabozho was helpful to human beings and taught them how to live. [*See also* MANABOZHO, ADVENTURES OF; NATIVE NORTH AMERICAN MYTHOLOGY.]

Manu (mä´ nü)

🐚 In INDIAN MYTHOLOGY, Manu is a name given to 14 different deities. Seven gods named Manu have existed so far; seven are yet to come. All are responsible for the CREATION of human beings at different times. [*See also* MANU AND THE FISH.]

Marduk (mär´ dük) ⟶ In BABY-
LONIAN MYTHOLOGY and ASSYRIAN
MYTHOLOGY, Marduk was a mighty
storm god and a great warrior. By
killing the goddess TIAMAT, he rose to
the top of the PANTHEON of gods. [*See
also ENUMA ELISH; TIAMAT; TRICKSTER.*]

Mars (märz) ⟶ *See* ARES.

Maui (mou´ ē) ⟶ Maui was a
great TRICKSTER god in POLYNESIAN
MYTHOLOGY. Maui's mother was the
Earth goddess Taranga. Because she
gave birth to Maui prematurely and
already had four sons, Taranga cast
the unformed child into the sea. Maui
was rescued by the Old Man of the
Sea, who raised him and told him

The god Marduk, shown on this seal,
was often mischievous and played
tricks.

Adventures of Manabozho
(mä nä bō´ zō)

Like most TRICKSTER characters in NATIVE
NORTH AMERICAN MYTHOLOGY, MANABOZHO was
powerful and kind but could also be foolish and
deceitful. According to some stories, as a baby
Manabozho (like GLOOSCAP) took immediate
revenge on a wolf brother who had killed their
mother. In other myths, his grandmother had
been exiled to earth from another world. Her
daughter was kidnapped by the West Wind and
died giving birth to Manabozho.

As Manabozho grew up, he became angry
about the way his father (the West Wind) had
treated his mother. When he was a young man
he set out to find his father. With every furious
step Manabozho grew larger and larger until
each of his strides covered miles. Manabozho
found the West Wind, outwitted him, and was
accepted as a son.

At that time, monsters still lived on the
earth. Manabozho came to help human beings,
who were terrorized by the monsters. Manabozho fought and killed many of them. One day
he was swallowed by a huge fish. He killed the
fish from the inside and eventually made his way
back to the world. Another time, great serpents
chased Manabozho up a tree and caused a FLOOD.
The tree stretched taller and taller, keeping
Manabozho above the rising water. Manabozho
survived the flood, but the land was still covered
by water. He asked for a bit of mud so he could
make new land. A muskrat finally succeeded in
diving beneath the water and bringing back
some mud for Manabozho. Manabozho magically
increased the mud and created new dry land.
Then he tracked down and killed the serpents
that had caused all the trouble. [*See also* EARTH
DIVER; MONSTER SLAYING.]

Manu and the Fish (mä´ nü)

In INDIAN MYTHOLOGY, the hero MANU survived a FLOOD with the help of a fish. One day Manu was washing his hands and discovered a small fish in the basin. The fish begged Manu for its life, promising to save Manu's life in return someday. Following the fish's instructions, Manu put the creature in larger and larger bodies of water as it grew. The fish eventually became enormous, and Manu finally put it in the ocean.

The fish then warned Manu of an impending deluge that would flood all the world. It told Manu to build a boat in which to save himself. Manu did so, and set sail in time to escape the rising waters. Manu tied a rope to a horn on the fish's head. The fish then towed Manu's boat to a mountaintop, where Manu tied the boat to a tree. When the floodwaters went down, Manu found himself the sole survivor in all the world. Manu sacrificed and prayed to the gods, who gave him a wife. Together, they started humankind anew. [*See also* APOCALYPSE.]

Mawu (mä´ wü) ● In the AFRICAN MYTHOLOGY of the Dahomey, Mawu was the high deity. Sometimes Mawu was male and sometimes female. The TRICKSTER character LEGBA was Mawu's son. According to many stories, Legba's pranks eventually caused Mawu to move away from the earth into the heavens.

Maya (mī´ ə) ● According to Buddhist INDIAN MYTHOLOGY, Maya was the mother of the Buddha, whom she conceived while dreaming of a white elephant. She died seven days after the birth of the Buddha, but was reborn in heaven. [*See also* REBIRTH AND RESURRECTION.]

Medea (mi dē´ ə) ● In GREEK MYTHOLOGY, Medea was a beautiful witch who helped JASON steal the golden fleece. She bore Jason two sons, but

stories of his own people. Maui grew curious to see his family for himself, so the sea god sent the boy home.

Like tricksters in other cultures, many of Maui's deeds helped humans. For example, he gave people speech and the gift of fire. But when he tried to trick the death goddess, he himself was killed. [*See also* MAUI, ADVENTURES OF.]

Indian gods such as Maya were often depicted in stone carvings.

he later deserted her to marry Glauce, the daughter of King Creon of Corinth. Medea murdered the bride and then killed her own children—partly for revenge against Jason and partly to save them from the consequences of her murder of Glauce.

Medea escaped from Corinth to Athens, where she became a great influence on King Aegeus. After trying unsuccessfully to murder Aegeus' son, THESEUS, Medea fled Athens and eventually returned to her home city of Colchis. [See also JASON AND THE GOLDEN FLEECE.]

This Roman bust of Medusa clearly shows the snakes writhing in her hair.

Maori Creation Myths (mou´ rē)

According to myths of the Maori of New Zealand, the world was created by Io, the supreme deity. At first there was only darkness and PRIMAL WATERS. Io spoke words to create the day and night. He separated the waters into heaven and earth. The spirit of the Heavens was the father, Rangi. The spirit of the Earth was the mother, whose name was Papa. The father and mother embraced each other so tightly that most of the children that were supposed to be born to them were trapped inside Papa.

One child named Tane was born. In some versions of the story Tane managed to separate his parents, but Rangi and Papa were miserable at being apart. Rangi's tears became the rain and Papa's sighs became the mist. Tane and one of his brothers created the insects, forests, and plants. Other siblings made the winds, rains, and earthquakes. One warrior god was the father of the Maori and another was the father of the god MAUI. In other myths, Tane became the god of life and created the Maori people from red clay.

In a variation of the Maori creation myth, Rangi and Papa had their children while the world was still dark. Locked in an embrace, they prevented the rest of CREATION from taking place. Light came into the world when the pair was separated, and then the creation of the world continued. [See also FATHER GOD; GREAT GODDESS; POLYNESIAN MYTHOLOGY; SEPARATION OF HEAVEN AND EARTH; WORLD PARENTS.]

Medusa (mi dü´ sə) ● Medusa was one of the gorgons in GREEK MYTHOLOGY. These were three sisters with claws, wings, and heads

Mayan Creation Myths (mī´ yən)

According to creation myths told in the Mayan book the *POPUL VUH*, the world was brought into being by words. Everything began with an empty sky and PRIMAL WATERS. As the gods of the sea and the sky talked, they created the earth, plants, and eventually people. During their dialogue, they brought the earth forth from the sea. They then set into motion the process of seeds growing into plants and the movements of the sun, moon, and stars.

The Mayan gods had to try four times before they created satisfactory human beings. On their first try, they made creatures without language, who became the ancestors of animals. The second time they made a living thing out of mud, but it could not hold its shape and eventually dissolved. They next tried to make humans out of wood. The humans could move and talk and multiply, but they were disorderly and forgot to pray. The gods sent both a flood and animal monsters to get rid of the wooden people.

The gods then had some adventures, in which hero twins named Hunahpu and Xbalanque made the world safer for the humans still to come. Finally, the gods made satisfactory humans from corn flour and water. This time they were so successful that the new people had perfect vision and perfect knowledge. After a discussion, the gods decided to fog human eyes so that people would not have such divine insight.

At this time, the world was still dark. As the earliest humans waited for light, they separated into tribes and learned different languages. Finally the morning star appeared, and then the sun. The coming of light brought a new unity to humankind, since they could now coordinate their lives in accord with the cycles of the calendar.

covered with snakes instead of hair. Of the three, Medusa alone was mortal. But she was still very hard to kill. One glance at a gorgon would turn a human to stone. Medusa was beheaded by the Greek hero PERSEUS. [*See also* MONSTER SLAYING; MONSTERS AND MYTHICAL BEASTS.]

Mercury (mer´ kyə rē) ❧ *See* HERMES.

Merlin (mer´ lin) ❧ In CELTIC MYTHOLOGY and ARTHURIAN LEGEND, Merlin was a magician and a prophet. He is said to have transported the stones for the ancient monument at Stonehenge and also to have founded the knighthood of the Holy Grail. Merlin is best known for being the teacher of the legendary King Arthur. [*See also* GRAIL QUEST.]

Monster Slaying ❧ Heroes in myths were often called upon to kill monsters. Sometimes they went in search of the monster, either to stop it from destroying people or to establish their own reputations as heroes. The monster slayer was usually rewarded with celebrity, a treasure, and sometimes a princess.

In some cases, heroes or heroines killed monsters in unusual ways. In NATIVE NORTH AMERICAN MYTHOLOGY, the TRICKSTER character COYOTE was once swallowed by a whale and had to cut his way out. The Blackfoot Indian hero KUTOYIS also killed the Wind Sucker monster from the inside. Then Kutoyis had to allow himself to

Adventures of Maui (mou´ē)

According to one version of the story of MAUI in POLYNESIAN MYTHOLOGY, he was the son of Taranga, an earth goddess, and the god Makea-tutara. Maui and his brothers saw Taranga only at night; she went away during the day but would not say where. One day, Maui secretly followed her through underground tunnels until they reached a lovely countryside. There Maui met many of his relatives, including his grandmother, Muri-ranga-whenua. He tricked his grandmother into giving him her jawbone, which he used on many of his adventures and also to create language.

On one occasion, Maui convinced his brothers to catch the fast-moving Sun in a net. Then Maui beat it with the jawbone. The poor, crippled Sun has limped through the sky ever since, making the days as long as they are now. At another time, Maui baited a hook with his own blood and made an extraordinary catch—large parts of the islands of New Zealand.

Maui stole fire from the goddess Mahu-ika, his great-great-grandmother. After he teased her for a long time, the goddess hurled fire at him, setting the world ablaze. Maui prayed until rain came, putting out all the fire except for a few sparks in some wood. Since then, wood has always been used in making fires.

Maui suffered a fatal defeat when he decided to trick Hina, the death goddess. While many animals watched, Maui crept over her body, intending to hit her on the head with his jawbone. Just when Maui reached her mouth, a bird laughed. The goddess's jaws snapped shut, killing Maui.

be killed, cooked, eaten, and resurrected four times before he could destroy a monster called Man Eater. KALI, the fierce goddess of INDIAN MYTHOLOGY, was not able to overcome the demon Raktavija with her weapons, so she killed the wounded monster by drinking all his blood. [*See also* ARIADNE; *BEOWULF;* CHANGING WOMAN; CYCLOPES; DANU; DISMEMBERMENT; DRAGONS; DURGA; *GILGAMESH;* GLOOSCAP; GRENDEL; HERCULES; INDRA; JASON; LABYRINTH; LITUOLONE; MANABOZHO; MEDUSA; NAVAJO TWINS; PERSEUS; RAMA; SIEGFRIED; THESEUS; TIAMAT.]

Monsters and Mythical Beasts

In myths from many cultures, fearsome imaginary creatures represented an evil power that a hero had to overcome. Such monsters and mythical beasts could be giant humans, animals, sea creatures, combinations of different animals, or combinations of animals and humans. Huge monsters called ogres were always hungry, especially for human flesh. Evil spirits called demons were held responsible for illness and other evils. In some tribal societies, demons

Mythical Beasts, such as this one at a temple in India, terrified people who heard stories about them.

were thought to be the hostile ghosts of dead ancestors. In INDIAN MYTHOLOGY, the goddess DANU gave birth to the demon Vritra, who was destroyed by the god INDRA. The Rakshas who kidnapped Sita, the wife of RAMA, were also demons.

While most monsters were evil, other mythical beasts—such as unicorns, centaurs, and winged horses—were less threatening or even helpful to people. A centaur was half man and half horse in GREEK MYTHOLOGY. Though often rowdy and coarse, a centaur named Chiron was a healer and a teacher who raised the hero JASON. [*See also* BALDER; *BEOWULF*; CHAOS; CUPID AND PSYCHE; CYCLOPES; DRAGONS; *GILGAMESH*; GLOOSCAP; GREEK CREATION MYTHS; GRENDEL; HERCULES; KALI; KUTOYIS; LABYRINTH; LILITH; LITUOLONE; MANABOZHO; MAYAN CREATION MYTHS; MEDUSA; MONSTER SLAYING; "ORPHEUS" THEME; QUEST; THESEUS; TIAMAT.]

Mountain ✎ Myths from around the world portray mountains as the source of supernatural powers and as sacred places where humans could communicate with deities. Mount Olympus, for example, was the home of the Greek PANTHEON. The Delphic Oracle of the Greek god APOLLO was on the slope of Mount Parnassus. (An oracle was a shrine where a priest or priestess spoke prophecies made by a god.) The golden mountain Meru was the home of the Hindu god SIVA.

In FLOOD stories, the survivors usually landed on a mountaintop,

In mythology, mountains often served as the home of gods.

Midir and Etain (mi dēr´) (e tān´)

The *LEABHAR GABHALA*, a collection of stories from CELTIC MYTHOLOGY, includes many tales about Midir and Etain. Midir was the god of the Underworld (a magical fairyland in these stories). Etain was the daughter of a king and the most beautiful maiden in Ireland. Midir insisted that Etain be his wife. But Midir's first wife, Fuamnach, turned Etain into a fly and tossed her into the wind.

For seven years, Etain was blown about helplessly. Then the fly fell into a golden goblet of wine, was swallowed by a woman, and was reborn as a new human being. Etain once more became the most beautiful maiden in Ireland. With no memory of her former life, she married King Eochaid.

When Midir found out where Etain was, he challenged King Eochaid to a game of chess. The winner could have whatever he desired. Midir lost the game on purpose and gave Eochaid 50 gray horses. He also performed several difficult tasks, including clearing the land of stones. Then Midir challenged the king to another chess game. Midir won and demanded Etain. When the king resisted, Midir and Etain flew away in the form of swans.

To get Etain back, King Eochaid's troops began digging into the fairy hill that covered the doorway to the Underworld. Midir sent out 50 fairy maidens, all of whom looked just like Etain, but Eochaid wanted only his true wife. To save his kingdom, Midir finally had to give Etain back to King Eochaid.

Midir waited angrily for Eochaid and Etain to have a son, so he could take revenge on him. But they had only daughters. Midir finally took his revenge on their great grandson, who died a violent death.

such as Parnassus in GREEK MYTHOLOGY. In many cultures, TEMPLES were based on the shape of mountains to symbolize their importance. This is evident in the pyramids of the Egyptians, Mayans, and Aztecs. [*See also* ANIMISM; *GILGAMESH*; KACHINAS; NATURE SPIRITS.]

Mwindo (mwēn´ dō) In the myths of Zaire in Africa, Mwindo was a name given to sons who were born after the family already had several daughters. Epic tales are told about characters named Mwindo who had unusual powers. For example, the unborn Mwindo could choose the time of his own birth, and he was born able to walk and talk. He was also born carrying a shoulder bag that held special objects, such as a rope, an ax, and other tools. Mwindo's magic tools responded to his commands and defended him whenever necessary. [*See also* AFRICAN MYTHOLOGY.]

Narcissus (när sis´ əs) ♒ In GREEK MYTHOLOGY, Narcissus was the son of a nymph (NATURE SPIRIT) and a river god. Narcissus became the handsomest young man in the world. But he fell in love with a reflection of himself in the water and killed himself when he could not reach this object of his desire. [*See also* NARCISSUS, DEATH OF.]

Native Central and South American Mythology ♒

Some common themes appear in myths from the many Central and

The handsome Narcissus lying next to the pool of water where he sees his reflection.

South American cultures. For example, the CREATION stories told in these cultures usually began with deities or a first ancestor already in existence. Aztec and Mayan myths say that several worlds existed before ours. According to many South American stories, the world was created by a magician who could transform reality.

Twins play major roles in stories from Central and South America. As in NATIVE NORTH AMERICAN MYTHOLOGY, Central and South American myths often include a TRICKSTER who helps humankind by providing fire or other benefits. Other myths describe the origins of the sun, moon, humans, animals, and other things in nature. [*See also* MAYAN CREATION MYTHS; *POPUL VUH*; QUETZACOATL.]

Native North American Mythology ♒

Stories from the Native American cultures of North America reflect the experience and values of many different Indian nations. They do have some common themes, including the EMERGENCE of humans onto the earth, deities who provide food and guidance for the people, and heroes and heroines who rescue those people from monsters.

Death of Narcissus (när sis´əs)

The handsome NARCISSUS was adored by many people. However, he returned no one's love and was not even very kind to those who cared for him.

The goddess HERA believed that her husband ZEUS was infatuated with a nymph, or nature goddess. Hera spied on the nymphs and she saw one named Echo chattering happily. Annoyed, Hera decreed that from then on Echo would only be able to repeat what others said to her.

Soon afterward, the unfortunate Echo fell madly in love with Narcissus. She followed him around, but he ignored her as he did all his admirers. Unable to tell Narcissus of her love, Echo faded away to a faint voice that can still be heard in the mountains and caves.

Finally, the prayers of someone that Narcissus had hurt reached a GREAT GODDESS (in some stories it is Artemis, in others Nemesis). The goddess decided that Narcissus might as well love himself, since he refused to love anyone else. One day while Narcissus was looking in a pool of water he saw his own reflection and fell in love with it. When he realized that it was his face and that he could not have this object of his desire, he was overcome with loneliness. He then stabbed himself, calling "Farewell!" to his reflection. Echo repeated, "Farewell!"

When Narcissus died, his body disappeared and a white flower appeared in his place. The flower was named Narcissus. [*See also* HYACINTHUS AND APOLLO.]

In some cases, stories about a descent to the Underworld include the "ORPHEUS" THEME of trying unsuccessfully to bring a loved one back. Other popular subjects include NATURE SPIRITS and powers that were believed to exist in the land itself, animal spirits, agricultural or FERTILITY figures, SHAMANS, and TRICKSTER gods.

Some Native North American myths can be traced back to Asian roots. In the EARTH DIVER stories, for example, a creature makes a difficult and dangerous dive into waters that covered the earth and brings back a bit of soil. Then a deity, usually a trickster, turns the soil into land. Similar stories, including the trickster, are found among the ancient myths of Japan, Mongolia, and Siberia. [*See also* ACOMA CREATION MYTH; APACHE CREATION MYTHS; BLACKFOOT ORPHEUS MYTH; CHANGING WOMAN; CHEROKEE CREATION MYTHS; CORN MOTHER; COYOTE; FROG AND WIYOT; GLOOSCAP; HOPI EMERGENCE; KACHINAS; KIOWA CREATION MYTHS; KUTOYIS; MANABOZHO; NAVAJO EMERGENCE; NAVAJO TWINS; OLD MAN; RAVEN; SEDNA; SIOUX CREATION MYTHS; SPIDER WOMAN; TREE THAT HOLDS UP THE WORLD; WATERJAR BOY; WHITE BUFFALO WOMAN; WIYOT; ZUNI CREATION MYTHS.]

The Haida Indians of North America often depicted nature spirits on totem poles and other objects.

Nature Spirits 🐦

According to many ancient myths, everything in nature contained a spirit (a living power or consciousness that inhabited a particular place, object, or natural element such as air or water). Stories from Japan, China, India, various Native North American peoples, and other cultures describe such spirits in the sun, moon, earth, sea, rivers, wind, stones, and living things. In the NATIVE NORTH AMERICAN MYTHOLOGY, for example, the Sioux told of a natural creative power called Wakan Tanka. Over a period of time, these spirits were often given names and

Navajo Emergence (nä´ və ho)

The myths of the Navajo Indians portray the CREATION of their world as an EMERGENCE from within the earth. This is common in NATIVE NORTH AMERICAN MYTHOLOGY. But the story of the Navajos is more complicated than most emergence stories. According to them, life passed through four underworlds before our own world came to be.

The earliest couple, First Woman and First Man, are sometimes said to have been born as ears of corn. They lived in the first underworld, where they planned and created Navajo culture. At first, this world was inhabited only by themselves, the TRICKSTER character called COYOTE, and insect peoples.

The peoples quarreled and fought, and their world was destroyed. So the earliest Navajos had to move to an underworld on top of the first. Three more times the peoples fought, and three more times another underworld had to be destroyed, either by fire or water. At last, the Navajos emerged into the their final world.

But human beings as we know them did not yet exist. They were created by CHANGING WOMAN, who had been raised by First Woman and First Man. She made the first four human couples from the sweaty waste of her skin. These people became the ancestors of today's Navajos. [*See also* APOCALYPSE; DYING GOD; FLOOD; MAYAN CREATION MYTHS; PERSEPHONE, HADES, AND DEMETER; REBIRTH AND RESURRECTION; WORLD PARENTS.]

developed into specific gods and goddesses whose stories were told in the mythology of each culture.

In GREEK MYTHOLOGY, nymphs were beautiful female nature spirits of trees, mountains, groves, caves, and so forth. Greek nymphs lived for thousands of years, but were not immortal. [*See also* ANIMISM; BALDER; CALYPSO; DIONYSUS; HANUMAN; JAPANESE CREATION MYTHS; KACHINAS; NARCISSUS; ODYSSEUS; SIOUX CREATION MYTHS.]

Navajo Twins (nä´ və hō)

In NATIVE NORTH AMERICAN MYTHOLOGY, the Navajo Twins killed monsters, or enemy gods, to make the world safer for human beings. They were the sons of CHANGING WOMAN, the Great Mother goddess of the Navajos. [*See also* GREAT GODDESS; MONSTERS AND MYTHICAL BEASTS; MONSTER SLAYING.]

Neptune *See* POSEIDON.

Nibelungenlied (nē´ bə lün gen lēd)

A German epic poem, the *Nibelungenlied* was written about A.D. 1200 by an unknown author. Based on Scandinavian and GERMANIC MYTHOLOGY, it was intended for performance at the royal court of Austria. The poem tells the story of the hero SIEGFRIED and BRYNHILD, a great woman warrior.

Siegfreid was a warrior prince who had once bathed in the blood of a dragon, making himself invulnerable except for one spot on his back where a leaf had fallen. He also had a magic cloak that made him invisible. Siegfried wanted to marry Kriemhild, the sister of King Gunther of Burgundy. Gunther was in love with Brynhild of Iceland, a woman with superhuman strength who had vowed to marry the man who could beat her in athletic competitions. Gunther offered Siegfried a deal: if he could get Brynhild to marry Gunther, then Siegfried could marry Kriemhild.

Siegfried used his magic cloak and deception to make it appear that Gunther won the competition. A double wedding was held. But on the wedding night, Brynhild grew suspicious of how Gunther had won and hung him on a hook. Gunther appealed to Siegfried, who put on his magic cape and wrestled Brynhild into submission. He took her girdle and ring and gave it to Kriemhild.

One day the two queens argued, and Kriemhild showed Brynhild the girdle and ring Siegfried had taken. A man named Hagen later tricked Kriemhild into revealing her husband's one vulnerable spot. Hagen murdered Siegfried, stole his treasure, and threw it into a river. Hagen and Kriemhild were later killed.

Nihongi (nē hōn´ gē)

JAPANESE MYTHOLOGY and early history are recorded in the *Kojiki* and the *Nihongi*—the earliest Japanese texts. Hiyeda no Are, believed to have been a woman, memorized both books and kept them in her head for 20 years. She wrote down the *Nihongi* in A.D. 720. [*See also* JAPANESE CREATION MYTHS.]

Norse Creation Myths (nôrs´)

In the Scandinavian CREATION story, at first there was only a great emptiness, or gap, called Ginnungagap. North of the gap, a dark, cold, foggy place called Nifhelm was formed. To the south was a hot area where a giant named Surt lived. Where the hot and cold air met, ice began to melt.

Drops of water from the melting ice formed a frost giant, named YMIR, his family, and a cow. The cow licked the ice, and the head of a man began to appear. After three days of licking, the cow had released a being named Buri from the ice.

Buri's son Bor married a frost giantess, and the god ODIN was one of their sons. After a long, fierce battle, the sons of Bor defeated the family of Ymir. Odin and his two brothers killed Ymir, and the giant's blood drowned most of the other frost giants.

Odin and his brothers created the world from Ymir's body. From the maggots in the dead giant's flesh, they made dwarfs called North, South, East, and West. From Ymir's eyebrows, they made Midgard, the earth where humans would live. They created the first man and woman, Ash and Elm, from fallen trees. Odin put the giants Night and Day into horse-drawn chariots and sent them to circle the world.

The three brothers also created Asgard, a beautiful home for themselves and the other gods. They connected Asgard to earth with a rainbow bridge. [*See also* DISMEMBERMENT; EDDAS; NORSE MYTHOLOGY; RAGNAROK, END OF THE WORLD.]

These stone carvings illustrate Norse myths of the Vikings.

Norse Mythology (nôrs´)

In ancient Scandinavian stories, poems, and songs, the Norse stories described nine worlds. Some were inhabited by gods, giants, dwarfs, or elves. Humans lived in Midgard, or middle earth. The land of the dead was ruled by the goddess Hel. The gods lived in a heavenly place called Asgard. Warriors who died in battle were taken to Valhalla, the hall of ODIN, by women warriors called Valkyries. [*See also* BALDER; EDDAS; FREYA; FRIGG; LOKI; NORSE CREATION MYTHS; RAGNAROK, END OF THE WORLD; YMIR.]

Odin (ō´ dən) 🐚

A mysterious god of NORSE MYTHOLOGY, Odin was the oldest of the Aesir, a group of warrior gods. Most of the Aesir were his children. Odin was considered the king of the gods, a god of war, and the creator of humans. He gave one of his eyes so that he could drink from the sacred well of Mirmir in order to gain wisdom. He also sacrificed himself, died, and was reborn to gain the secrets of the dead. Warriors who die in battle were brought to Odin's great hall, Valhalla, where they were to form an army to fight for him at RAGNAROK, END OF THE WORLD. [*See also* ODIN, TRIALS OF.]

The god Odin, shown in this stone figure, was one of the most powerful Norse gods.

Odysseus (ō dis´ē əs) 🐚

A hero in GREEK MYTHOLOGY, ODYSSEUS was a famous king of Ithaca who fought in the Trojan War and experienced many adventures on his way home after the war. Known as much for his wiliness and cleverness as for his courage, Odysseus often defeated his opponents more through shrewdness than physical strength. He appears in two works by the Greek poet Homer—the *ILIAD*, a story of the Trojan War, and the *ODYSSEY*, a story about his adventures after the war. Odysseus is known as Ulysses in ROMAN AND ETRUSCAN MYTHOLOGY. [*See also* ODYSSEUS, ADVENTURES OF.]

Trials of Odin (ō´ dən)

The god ODIN of NORSE MYTHOLOGY was both the FATHER GOD who created the world and a war god. In some stories he was also the god of poetry, wisdom, or death. Although usually pictured with a long white beard and a wide-brimmed hat he could change his shape and often traveled through his kingdom in disguise.

Odin and his wife, FRIGG, were the parents of the gods called the Aesir. They lived in Asgard, the dwelling place of the gods. From the throne in one of his palaces, Odin could see everything in his worlds. He had two ravens who brought him news of his kingdom, and also two wolves. His magic spear, Grungnir, never missed its target. His eight-legged horse, Sleipnir, could fly through the air and could travel to the Underworld. Odin's other palace, called Valhalla, was where human warriors who died bravely in battle came to rest.

Odin had a great desire for knowledge and twice endured great pain to get it. To better understand the universe, Odin crucified himself for nine nights on Yggdrasil, the World Tree. As he suffered from a spear wound, hunger, and thirst, his wisdom grew. Odin learned the runes, a secret alphabet with magic powers.

Odin also sacrificed one eye to gain knowledge. The mead in the Well of Mimer brought wisdom to anyone who drank it. (Mead is an alcoholic drink made from honey and water.) For a drink of his mead, Mirmer demanded the price of an eye. After drinking the magic mead, Odin could see that the world would end in a great battle called RAGNAROK, END OF THE WORLD. He knew that he would die there, swallowed by a wolf who was the son of LOKI. [*See also* BALDER; BRYNHILD; FREYA; GERMANIC MYTHOLOGY; NORSE CREATION MYTHS; SIEGFRIED; YMIR.]

Odyssey (ä d´ ə sē) 🐚 An epic poem by the Greek poet Homer, the *Odyssey* describes the adventures of the hero ODYSSEUS after the Trojan War. Compiled from many Greek myths and folktales, the poem was composed around the ninth century B.C. [*See also* GREEK MYTHOLOGY.]

Oedipus (ed´ ə pus) 🐚 According to GREEK MYTHOLOGY, Oedipus was born in Thebes, the son of King Laius and Queen Jocasta. When a prophet warned that the baby would one day kill his father, Laius left Oedipus on a mountainside to die.

The child was rescued by a shepherd and adopted by the king and queen of Corinth. When he grew older, Oedipus heard from a prophet that he would kill his father and marry his mother. Believing that this meant his foster parents, Oedipus fled Corinth. While traveling, he

Adventures of Odysseus (ō dis´ ē əs)

The hero ODYSSEUS joined the Greek forces in their war against Troy. After ten years of fighting, Odysseus had the Greeks build a huge wooden horse. He and several other warriors hid inside the horse's belly, and the Trojans took the horse into the city. Late that night, Odysseus and his companions crept out of the horse and opened the city gates, bringing about the downfall of Troy.

With the end of the war, the Greek army sailed for home. However, a great storm blew the ships bearing Odysseus and his men off course. For ten years, Odysseus wandered the world, encountering many strange lands and peoples.

In the land of the lotus-eaters, some of Odysseus' men ate a magical plant that made them forget their homes. Odysseus found it difficult to make them leave. On another island, Odysseus outwitted and blinded the man-eating CYCLOPES. He and his followers then continued their travels to the land of the sorceress CIRCE. She turned Odysseus' men into swine, but he managed to break this spell.

Uncertain how to get home after many years of travel, Odysseus went to the Underworld to ask the advice of a dead prophet named Tiresias. Following Tiresias' directions, Odysseus and his crew faced further dangers, including the Sirens, strange creatures who lured sailors to their deaths with their singing. Before Odysseus reached home, he was captured by the sea nymph CALYPSO. She held him prisoner for seven years until the god ZEUS ordered her to set him free.

When ODYSSEUS finally arrived home in Ithaca, he found his palace overrun by suitors determined to marry his wife, PENELOPE. ODYSSEUS and his son Telemachus slew the suitors, and ODYSSEUS ruled Ithaca wisely from that time on. [*See also AENEID; ODYSSEY; UNDERWORLD, DESCENT TO.*]

Odysseus is shown here with Calypso, who kept him prisoner on her island.

unwittingly murdered his real father. He then became king of Thebes and married Jocasta, his real mother. Upon learning the truth about his deeds, Oedipus blinded himself. [*See also* TRIALS AND TESTS.]

Okanagon Mother (ō kan ä´ gən) In the myths of the Okanagon Indians of what is now the northwestern United States, the creator made the earth from a human woman. Her hair became trees and plants, her flesh became soil, her bones became rocks, and her breath became the wind. He also made the first people from her flesh. Though changed, the woman known as Okanagon Mother is still alive. When she gets restless, there is an earthquake. [*See also* CREATION; DISMEMBERMENT; GAIA; GREAT GODDESS; NATIVE NORTH AMERICAN MYTHOLOGY.]

Old Man In NATIVE NORTH AMERICAN MYTHOLOGY, a great spirit, teacher, and TRICKSTER hero called Old Man appeared in stories told by the Blackfoot, Arapaho, Algonquin, Sioux, and other Indian peoples. In some myths he was the creator of the world, including humans and animals. In others, Old Man also taught people how to make babies.

Orpheus (ôr´ fē əs) In GREEK MYTHOLOGY, Orpheus was a great musician who played so well that he could charm rivers, trees, and stones. He was the son of Calliope, one of the Muses, the nine patron god-

desses of the arts and sciences. His father was Oeager, sometimes said to be the son of the war god ARES. [*See also* ORPHEUS AND EURYDICE.]

"Orpheus" Theme (ôr´ fē əs) In GREEK MYTHOLOGY, the poet and musician ORPHEUS failed to bring his wife EURYDICE back from the Underworld because he disobeyed the command not to look back at her. This theme—a trip to the Underworld and disobedience of the rules—also appears in myths from other cultures. In the NATIVE NORTH AMERICAN MYTHOLOGY of the Nez Percé Indians,

This ancient Roman mosaic shows Orpheus charming animals with his lyre, or harp.

Orpheus and Eurydice (ôr´ fē əs) (yủ rid´ ə sē)

According to GREEK MYTHOLOGY, the great musician ORPHEUS married EURYDICE, a dryad, or nymph (NATURE SPIRIT). But she was bitten by a snake and died almost immediately after their wedding. Grief-stricken, Orpheus was determined to bring her back from the Underworld.

The living are not normally allowed in the realm of the dead. But Orpheus played his lyre so beautifully that he charmed the guardians of the Underworld. Once there, Orpheus sang and played to HADES and PERSEPHONE, the king and queen of the Underworld. Unable to resist his music, they agreed to let Eurydice return to the world of living.

Orpheus was allowed to lead Eurydice out of the Underworld. But he was warned not to look back at her until they both had emerged into the world of the living. Orpheus obeyed this command until he himsel stepped into the sunlight. Then, unthinkingly, he glanced back. Eurydice, who had not yet emerged into the sunlight, was immediately taken back to the Underworld. Heartbroken, Orpheus went off to play his music alone.

A band of maenads— female followers of DIONYSUS—found Orpheus and tried to attract him. But Orpheus was no longer interested in mortal women, so the maenads tore him limb from limb. The pieces of his body were gathered up by the Muses, the nine patron goddesses of the arts and sciences. They buried Orpheus at the foot of Mount Olympus. ZEUS, the king of the gods, placed Orpheus' lyre in the sky as a constellation. And Orpheus' ghost was reunited with that of his beloved Eurydice in the AFTERLIFE. [See also JOURNEY QUEST; "ORPHEUS" THEME; UNDERWORLD, DESCENT TO.]

the Underworld spirits let COYOTE take his dead wife back. He was told not to touch her until they arrived, but he forgot and embraced her. She immediately vanished.

In a Japanese variation of the Orpheus theme, Izanagi found his wife, Izanami, in the Underworld, but when he looked at her there she was enraged. Monsters chased Izanagi back to the surface. [See also BLACK-FOOT ORPHEUS MYTH; ORPHEUS AND EURYDICE; UNDERWORLD, DESCENT TO.]

Osiris (ō sī´ rəs) In EGYPTIAN MYTHOLOGY, Osiris was the grandson of the Sun God RA. His parents were the Sky Goddess Nut and the Earth God Geb. The ruler over death, Osiris was also the god of vegetation. He and his wife and sister ISIS brought civilization to Egypt. Their story is recorded in the BOOK OF THE DEAD and other ancient Egyptian texts. [See also GEB AND NUT; HORUS; OSIRIS, DEATH AND RESURRECTION OF; SETH.]

Death and Resurrection of Osiris (ō sī´ rəs)

When Osiris and ISIS ruled Egypt, they built towns and made laws. Osiris showed people how to grow food, use wild fruit, and make wine and beer. Isis taught them to grind grain, bake bread, and weave.

Osiris' reign was peaceful. But his brother SETH was jealous of him. Seth invited Osiris and Isis to a banquet. He showed them a golden coffin and said he would give it to Osiris if he could fit into it. When Osiris got in the coffin, Seth slammed the lid shut and threw it into the Nile River.

Osiris drowned, and the gold box was swept across the Mediterranean Sea. Where the coffin landed, a tree quickly grew up around it. The tree gave off a wonderful perfume. A king and queen of the land of Byblos found the tree and had it made into a pillar for their great hall. They did not know a coffin was inside it.

Isis went searching for her husband's body. When she arrived at Byblos, she heard stories of the great tree that supported the royal hall and gave off a won-derful perfume. Isis went to see the tree and recognized the odor as her husband's favorite scent. The king and queen of Byblos helped her remove the coffin from the tree and put it on a ship. Isis sailed for home, stopping to search for herbs to bring Osiris back to life. Crocodiles told Seth what Isis was doing. He came and chopped the body of Osiris into pieces and scattered them far and wide.

Isis searched until she found all the pieces of Osiris' body. She put them together, used her herbs, and wrapped the body in linen. Osiris then returned to life, but he no longer felt at home in the land of the living. After the growing season ended, he went to live in the Under-world. Each year since, Osiris returns to Egypt for the growing season and then goes back to the Underworld. [*See also BOOK OF THE DEAD*; DISMEMBERMENT; DYING GOD; EGYPTIAN MYTHOLOGY; FER-TILITY MYTHS; LEMMINKAINEN'S DEATH AND RESURRECTION; TREE.]

The god Osiris was one of the most important gods of ancient Egypt.

P

Pandavas (pän´ dä väs) 🪶

In INDIAN MYTHOLOGY, the Pandavas were five heroic brothers. The mythical Pandavas were referred to as the children of gods or as the incarnations (embodiments in human form) of gods on earth. The best-known brother was Arjuna, the general of the Pandava army. Arjuna was sometimes identified as an incarnation of the god VISNU. The Pandavas' story appears in the *MAHABHARATA*. A section of the *Mahabharata* called the *Bhagavad Gita* is a dialogue between Arjuna and the god KRISHNA about how human beings should live. [*See also* DRAUPADI; PANDAVAS, WAR OF THE.]

Pandora (pan dōr´ ə) 🪶 In GREEK MYTHOLOGY, Pandora was the first woman, and the mother of all other women. She was formed out of clay by the god of fire, HEPHAESTUS. Like EVE, the first woman in the Bible, Pandora was very curious, and her curiosity caused great problems for humankind. [*See also* PANDORA'S BOX;]

Pantheons (pan´ thē´ äns) 🪶 In ancient civilizations in which people believed in many Gods and goddesses, the most important deities formed a collective group known as a pantheon, a word that means "all gods." Temples dedicated to all of the gods were called Pantheons.

In GREEK MYTHOLOGY, the 12 gods and goddesses who lived on Mount Olympus belonged to the Olympic pantheon. The Romans adopted many Greek deities, but they changed some names. The Roman pantheon was

Despite the problem she caused, Pandora was revered by ancient Greeks and Romans.

War of the Pandavas

An Indian epic, the *MAHABHARATA*, tells the story of a great battle between the Pandava brothers and their cousins, the Kauravas. According to Indian mythology, the Kauravas were demons, and the battle became the cousins' divine plan to cleanse the world of evil.

One Pandava brother, Arjuna, was reluctant to fight. He told his concerns to KRISHNA, who was his charioteer. Victory would be won at great cost, Arjuna explained. He would have to kill his own kinsmen, which would damage the order of society. And war always produced lawlessness and corruption. Besides that, ruling the world would be very difficult. Arjuna was tempted to allow himself to be killed without resistance.

A section of the *Mahabharata* called the *Bhagavad Gita* is Krishna's lengthy reply to Arjuna. Krishna revealed that he was a deity, an embodiment on earth of the god VISNU. Krishna told Arjuna how humans should live in order to know God. Krishna said that it was Arjuna's duty to fight in this war of righteousness. No matter what was destroyed by the war, Krishna said, Arjuna should remember that his soul was indestructible. Arjuna entered the battle, and the Pandavas defeated the demons, ridding the world of much evil. [*See also* DRAUPADI; MONSTERS AND MYTHICAL BEASTS.]

therefore very similar to that of the Greeks. In the Americas, the Aztec and Mayan pantheons also had some parallel deities, notably the feathered serpent identified as QUETZALCOATL by the Aztecs and Kukulcan by the Maya. In the pantheon of EGYPTIAN MYTHOLOGY, the gods were involved in a strugle for supremacy. In NORSE MYTHOLOGY, the god ODIN ruled the other deities of the pantheon. The many gods of the Hindu pantheon are sometimes described in INDIAN MYTHOLOGY as different aspects of the one god, BRAHMA. [*See also* ROMAN AND ETRUSCAN MYTHOLOGY; POLYNESIAN MYTHOLOGY.]

Parvati (pär vä´ tē) ◈

One form taken by the GREAT GODDESS Devi in INDIAN MYTHOLOGY, Parvati is sometimes depicted with four arms. She was a fertility goddess as well as the devoted wife of the god SIVA. Parvati's marriage to Siva was not always easy. For one thing, Siva did not want children. Since Parvati did, she created her son GANESA without her husband's help. Their story appears in the *RAMAYANA*. [*See also* FERTILITY MYTHS.]

Parvati was a gentle goddess.

Pele (pē´ lē) 🐚 In POLYNESIAN MYTHOLOGY, Pele was a beautiful goddess of fire and volcanoes. Not surprisingly for a deity associated with heat and lava, she was known to be very passionate and temperamental. When Pele became angry, her fury could set fire to all those around her. She was often said to live in Hawaii, having journeyed there by canoe from Tahiti during her long search for her husband. Pele's stories were traditionally told in ritual chants and in the sacred dance called the hula. [*See also* PELE, THE JOURNEY OF.]

Penelope (pə nel´ ə pē) 🐚 In GREEK MYTHOLOGY, Penelope was the

Penelope, the faithful wife of Odysseus, waited 20 years for her husband's return.

Pandora's Box (pan dōr´ ə)

According to GREEK MYTHOLOGY there once was a time called the Golden Age during which the only human beings in the world were men. They lived happy, blessed lives, thanks largely to the Titan PROMETHEUS, who had given them fire.

ZEUS, the king of the gods, was not pleased with human happiness and decided to put an end to it. Zeus ordered his fellow gods to create the first woman. Her name was PANDORA, which meant "the gift of all." The gods gave Pandora a mysterious box that they forbade her to open.

Pandora was very beautiful, and Prometheus' brother Epimetheus fell in love with her. Prometheus had warned Epimetheus never to accept gifts from the gods, but Epimetheus married Pandora anyway. She became the mother of all women.

Unfortunately, Pandora had a tremendous curiosity and could not resist opening the box the gods had given her. When she did, out came all the evils that plague humankind, including disease, madness, work, and old age. Pandora slammed the box lid shut, but it was too late. Only one thing remained inside the box, and that was hope. According to most versions of the story, this suggests that hope is always present in our lives.

wife of ODYSSEUS. Because of his long absence after the Trojan War, people thought she must be a widow. Many men wanted to marry her, but Penelope continued to believe that Odysseus would return. She promised her suitors that she would marry one

The Journey of Pele (pā´ lā)

In POLYNESIAN MYTHOLOGY, the beautiful but temperamental goddess Pele is usually said to inhabit the volcano Kilauea on the island of Hawaii. Pele originally lived in Tahiti, but she was forced to leave because of her frequently harsh behavior. She traveled north in search of a new home, arriving at the Hawaiian islands.

Pele burrowed and dug into the island of Kaula, trying to build herself a dwelling place. But the ocean flooded in and ruined her work. She ran into similar problems at the islands of Lehua, Niihau, Kauai, Oahu, Molokai, Lanai, and Maui. At last, on the island of Hawaii, Pele succeeded in excavating a home for herself in Kilauea. Because of Pele's presence there, Kilauea is often described in Polynesian myths as "the navel of the earth."

In another well-known story about Pele, she once took human form and won the love of the handsome chief of Kauai, named Lohiau. They were married but Pele soon left Lohiau, promising that she would send for him. Lohiau waited and waited, but no one came. He finally died of grief. Pele finally sent her sister Hiiaka to bring Lohiau to her, but when Hiiaka got to Kauai she first had to bring the dead chief back to life.

Pele, meanwhile, became certain that her sister had fallen in love with Lohiau. By the time the two arrived, Pele was so jealous that she burst into flames, turning Lohiau into lava that hardened into stone. Hiiaka went to the Underworld to find Lohiau's soul. With the help of other gods, Lohiau was eventually returned to life. He returned to his own island, taking Hiiaka with him. [*See also* JOURNEY QUEST.]

of them as soon as she finished weaving a shroud (a cloth used to wrap a body for burial) for her father-in-law. Penelope wove during the day but never seemed to finish the shroud. Finally the suitors caught her unraveling her work at night. They became more determined than ever, so Penelope said that she would marry the one who could pass a test. He had to string Odysseus' bow, which was too strong for any ordinary man to bend, and shoot an arrow through 12 rings lined up in a row. Penelope discovered that Odysseus had reached home at last when he, in disguise, passed the test. [*See also* ODYSSEUS; *ODYSSEY*.]

Perceval (pėr´ sə väl) *See* ARTHURIAN LEGEND.

Persephone (pėr sef´ ə nē)
The daughter of DEMETER and ZEUS in GREEK MYTHOLOGY, Persephone liked to pick flowers. One day, while she was gathering flowers in Sicily, the earth opened up as she picked a particularly lovely bloom. She was then carried away to the Underworld by the god HADES and became his queen. In some stories, Persephone, known by the Romans as Proserpina, was the protector of DIONYSUS when he was a child. [*See also* PERSEPHONE, HADES, AND DEMETER.]

Perseus (pėr´ sē əs) A hero in GREEK MYTHOLOGY, Perseus was the son of the god ZEUS and Danaë, a mortal woman. Danaë's father, King

A Roman sculpture from the 400s B.C. shows Persephone and Hades on thrones in the Underworld.

Acrisius of Argos, had heard from a prophet that his grandson would someday kill him. So Acrisius put Danaë and the baby Perseus in a chest and set them adrift at sea.

The chest washed ashore on the island of Seriphus, where Perseus grew to manhood. Polydectes, the king of Seriphus, fell in love with Danaë, but wanted her son out of the way. So he sent Perseus on what seemed certain to be a fatal mission. This was to kill the gorgon MEDUSA, the sight of whose face turned people to stone.

Perseus succeeded and killed Medusa. He used the monster's head to rescue Andromeda, the princess of

This Roman sculpture shows Perseus beheading Medusa.

Ethiopia, from a sea monster by showing it Medusa's head and turning the creature to stone. Then Perseus turned King Polydectes and his court to stone as well and married Andromeda. The hero HERCULES was the great-grandson of Perseus and Andromeda.

Eventually, Perseus accidentally killed Acrisius during an athletic competition. He threw a discus that fatally struck the elderly king, fulfilling the old prophesy at last. [*See also* JOURNEY QUEST; MONSTER SLAYING; QUEST.]

Phan Ku (fan´ kü´) ✎ In CHINESE CREATION MYTHS, Phan Ku was the first being. He separated the heavens from the earth and shaped the earth itself with a hammer and a chisel. After Phan Ku died, his remains brought life to his CREATION. In another version of the story, Phan Ku

Persephone, Hades, and Demeter
(pėr sefʹə nē) (hādʹ ēz) (di mētʹ ėr)

The goddess DEMETER adored her daughter PERSEPHONE. But HADES, the god of the Underworld, kidnapped the girl and took her to his dark realm.

Demeter wandered the world searching for her daughter. Disguised as an elderly beggar woman, she arrived in the village of Eleusis. There she was taken in and cared for by Celeus and his wife Metaneira. Demeter tried to make their baby, Triptolemus, immortal by secretly placing him in a hot bed of coals. But Metaneira observed this rite and screamed in horror. Angry, Demeter revealed herself as a goddess and refused to immortalize the baby. But she promised that Triptolemus would grow up to be an important priest.

The people of Eleusis built Demeter a TEMPLE, where she lived and continued to mourn for her daughter. The Earth mourned along with her. Everything died, including all crops and livestock. The human race was in danger of extinction.

ZEUS, the king of the gods, persuaded his brother Hades to let Persephone return to the living. But before Persephone departed, Hades offered her a pomegranate, and she ate some of its seeds. To eat any food in the Underworld meant one would never be able to leave—at least not for good. So Persephone had to return to Hades' realm from time to time.

Persephone and her mother were joyfully reunited for eight months. During that time, the earth bloomed and there was plenty to eat. But then it came time for her to return to her husband Hades. Persephone remained with him for four months, and the earth withered with Demeter's sadness. And so it happens every year that the earth experiences a season of fruitfulness and a season when plants wither and die.

Demeter was worshipped in Eleusis, and Triptolemus grew up to be her first great priest. He spread the knowledge of farming and grain throughout the world . [*See also* FERTILITY MYTHS; REBIRTH AND RESURRECTION; UNDERWORLD, DESCENT TO.]

was a giant who was cut up to form the world. [*See also* DISMEMBERMENT; SEPARATION OF HEAVEN AND EARTH.]

Pluto ☙ *See* HADES.

Polynesian Mythology
(päl ə nēʹ zhən) ☙ Myths from the cultures of the Polynesian islands vary greatly. They reflect the different cultures themselves, which are spread throughout the Pacific Ocean in places like New Zealand, Hawaii, Tahiti, and Samoa.

In many Polynesian stories, the creator god TA'AROA was at the top of the PANTHEON of gods. A goddess of death, Hina, was often associated with tapa, a material used in clothing. MAUI was a TRICKSTER deity, Tane was a god of forests, and PELE was a goddess of fire and volcanoes.

In addition to telling about the CREATION of the world and humankind, Polynesian myths touch upon realities of island life—especially the ocean and volcanoes. Polynesian societies have often been structured according to their myths, with chiefs claiming descent from the gods. Important chiefs have been raised to the rank of gods after their deaths. [*See also* HAWAIIAN CREATION MYTHS.]

Popul Vuh (pō pül vü)

Ancient Mayan history and mythology is described in the *Popul Vuh*. The stories include heroes, deities, and the CREATION of the universe. This book was written in the European alphabet around the mid-1500s. However, the stories are much older and were originally told orally or were written in Mayan hieroglyphs. [*See also* MAYAN CREATION MYTHS; NATIVE CENTRAL AND SOUTH AMERICAN MYTHOLOGY.]

Poseidon (pō sīd´ ən)

The brother of ZEUS and HADES in GREEK MYTHOLOGY, Poseidon ruled the sea with the goddess Amphitrite as his queen. He is said to have given the first horse to humankind, and horses were sacred to him. He was also known as the "Earth-shaker" because he could cause earthquakes with his

trident, a long-handled three-pronged spear. According to some stories, Poseidon, rather than King Aegeus, was the father of the Greek hero THESEUS. [*See also* GREEK CREATION MYTHS.]

Primal Waters (pri´ məl)

According to some CREATION myths, at the beginning of time there was nothing but endless water. Then a deity appeared and separated the earth from the water. The primal waters usually represented the female principle, which gave birth to life. In ancient EGYPTIAN CREATION MYTHS, this primal ocean was CHAOS, or Nun. In BABYLONIAN MYTHOLOGY it was TIAMAT.

The Greek god Poseidon was known as Neptune by the Romans.

Deeds of Prometheus (prō mē´ thē əs)

The Titan PROMETHEUS sided with ZEUS and the Olympian gods when they rebelled against the Titans. So, for a time, he was Zeus' ally. But Prometheus is especially famous for helping humankind. In doing so, however, he often found himself at odds with Zeus, the ruler of the Olympian gods.

According to one story, Prometheus and his brother Epimetheus created human beings out of clay and water. The brothers also gave out skills and strengths to all the earth's creatures. Not nearly as wise as his brother, Epimetheus quickly gave everything away to the animals, leaving nothing good for the people. To make up for this lack, Prometheus tricked Zeus into accepting fat and bones as sacred sacrifices, while humans were allowed to eat meat.

Prometheus also brought fire down from the sun and gave it to humankind.

This was Prometheus' most famous and valuable gift to people—and the one which got him into the most trouble. Furious with Prometheus for stealing the fire, Zeus ordered him chained to a rock in the Caucasus Mountains. An eagle came daily and feasted on Prometheus' liver, which grew back again and again. The wretched Titan suffered like this for 30,000 years. At last, the Greek hero HERCULES arrived, slew the eagle, and then freed Prometheus.

Prometheus also helped humankind when Zeus sought to destroy all people by a FLOOD. When Prometheus learned of Zeus' plan, he instructed his son Deucalion and his niece Pyrrha to hide in a wooden chest. The chest floated until the floodwaters subsided, and Deucalion and Pyrrha created the human race anew from earth and stone. [*See also* PANDORA'S BOX.]

Many creation stories in NATIVE NORTH AMERICAN MYTHOLOGY began with primal water. In some cases, a few birds and animals existed before the land was formed. One of them became an EARTH DIVER who brought the deity the first bit of mud used to form the land. [*See also* APACHE CREATION MYTHS; CHEROKEE CREATION MYTHS; DANU; EGYPTIAN CREATION MYTHS; FINNIC CREATION MYTHS; JAPANESE CREATION MYTHS; LONE MAN AND THE MANDAN CREATION; MAORI CREATION MYTHS; MAYAN CREATION MYTHS; SKY GIRL; WORLD PARENTS.]

Prometheus (prō mē´ thē əs)

In GREEK MYTHOLOGY, Prometheus was a Titan—one of the giants who ruled the universe before ZEUS and the other Olympian gods came to power. His name means "forethought," and he was known for his great wisdom. He had a foolish brother named Epimetheus, which means "afterthought." Prometheus was punished by Zeus for ridiculing the Olympian gods and stealing fire from the sun. [*See also* PANDORA'S BOX; PROMETHEUS, DEEDS OF.]

Q R

Quest (kwest´) 🐚 Myths from around the world describe long, difficult searches called quests, which are undertaken by heroes and heroines. Many quests were to find people, places, magical objects, or information important to an entire nation. In ARTHURIAN LEGEND, all the knights of the Round Table vowed to undertake a quest for a sacred object, the Holy Grail, which was said to be the cup Christ used at the Last Supper.

More personal quests were for such things as youth, wisdom, or spirituality. The quest of Gilgamesh, for example, was for eternal life. Many such quests were internal. The Ojibwa Indian hero Wunzh prayed and fasted alone in the woods to discover a new source of food. As a result of his successful quest, Wunzh brought corn to his people and taught them how to grow and prepare it.

Severe TRIALS AND TESTS usually awaited those who went on quests. They often had to fight MONSTERS AND MYTHICAL BEASTS, such as the man-eating CYCLOPES that menaced AENEAS during his quest for a new city. While facing such trials, heroes often had to overcome flaws in their own character as well. [*See also*

AENEAS; DREAMING; *GILGAMESH;* GRAIL QUEST; HERO AND HEROINE; JASON AND THE GOLDEN FLEECE; JOURNEY QUEST; MONSTER SLAYING; NAVAJO TWINS; ORPHEUS AND EURYDICE; "ORPHEUS" THEME; PERSEUS; *RAMAYANA;* SIBYL; WANJIRU; WATER-JAR BOY.]

This stained glass window shows Sir Galahad, a knight of King Arthur's roundtable, on a quest for the Holy Grail.

Quetzalcoatl Saga (ket säl kō ät´ əl)

In the mythology of the Aztecs of Mexico, Quetzalcoatl was known as the feathered serpent. His name was a combination of *quetzal* (a rare, brightly feathered bird) and the word for snake. He was also a human priest, or perhaps several priests with the same name. There were many variations on the myths about Quetzalcoatl, and the historical and divine figures merged in them.

During his earthly rule, Quetzalcoatl brought civilization to his people. He invented the calendar and taught human beings how to grow corn and prepare it for food. His reign was a happy time for the Aztecs, during which agriculture was successful and food was plentiful. The priest Quetzalcoatl was too kindhearted to allow human or animal SACRIFICE, even when his sorcerers requested it.

The Aztecs believed that the universe had been created and destroyed a number of times. In one CREATION story, the god Quetzalcoatl made a hazardous trip to the Underworld to obtain the bones of earlier humans. He mixed the ground bones with his own blood and created the people who live in our world.

For reasons that vary in different stories, Quetzalcoatl eventually left his people. Some say that he was coaxed by demons into a drunken orgy so alien to his true nature that he left in shame. Others say that enemies drove him away, possibly because of his refusal to sacrifice living beings. Like ARTHURIAN LEGEND, Aztec myths predict the return of their great ruler. In 1519, the Spanish explorer Hernan Cortes landed on the Mexican shore. Because it was the calendar day of Quetzalcoatl's birth, the Aztec king Montezuma II believed that Quetzalcoatl had returned. [*See also* MAYAN CREATION MYTHS; NATIVE CENTRAL AND SOUTH AMERICAN MYTHOLOGY; UNDERWORLD, DESCENT TO.]

Quetzalcoatl was one of the most popular figures in the art of ancient Mexico.

Quetzalcoatl (ket säl kō ät´ əl)

The god of arts, crafts, and self-sacrifice in the Aztec myths of ancient Mexico, Quetzalcoatl was also a human priest. Stories about Quetzalcoatl were written in Aztec records and books called codexes. In some stories, he sprang from a jewel swallowed by a Moon Goddess. In others, his father was the Sun. Quetzalcoatl appeared in myths of the Toltec people of Mexico several hundred years before the fourteenth-century Aztec legends from which he is best known. NATIVE CENTRAL AND SOUTH AMERICAN MYTHOLO-

GY was always rich in wordplay. Quetzalcoatl also represented water and, in addition to that, the name implied twins. [*See also* QUETZALCOATL SAGA.]

Ra (rä) 🐚 In EGYPTIAN MYTHOLOGY, Ra was the Sun God. All earthly creatures were born from his tears. As Ra aged, gods and people took advantage of his feebleness, so he left earth to travel the heavens and the Underworld for all eternity. He was said to be the ancestor of the Egyptian pharaohs.

Rama (räm´ä) 🐚 The hero of INDIAN MYTHOLOGY recorded in the *RAMAYANA*, Rama was an avatar (incarnation on earth) of the Hindu god VISNU. When Rama's wife SITA was kidnapped by demons, Rama went on a long and dangerous QUEST to get her back. [*See also* RAMA'S QUEST FOR SITA.]

The god Rama was known for his heroic actions.

Ragnarok, End of the World
(rag´ nə räk)

According to NORSE MYTHOLOGY, the world will end at an APOCALYPSE called Ragnarok. One of the signs that Ragnarok is near will be the death of the best-loved god, BALDER.

According to the Norse stories, just before Ragnarok comes, the sun will grow dim and evil forces will be released. A terrible, final battle will involve gods, giants, and other creatures of great power. There will be three awful winters with no summers in between, during which there will be a war among the humans who live in Midgard. The morning of Ragnarok, three roosters will crow to rouse the giants, the dead in Hel, and the dead warriors in Valhalla, the great hall of ODIN. The god Heimdall will sound a blast on his horn, and the final battle will begin.

During the final battle, LOKI will lead the giants against the gods in Asgard, the beautiful home of the gods. Odin, wearing a golden helmet and carrying his magic sword, will lead the dead warriors from Valhalla. Powerful giant wolves will run free. One will swallow the sun; another will destroy the moon. A wolf named Fenrir will swallow Odin. Then Fenrir will be killed by Odin's son, Vidar. The warriors of Valhalla will be defeated and Asgard will be destroyed.

After the battle, the giant Surt will burn everything in the world. The earth will vanish into the sea. However, Ragnarok will not be the end of everything. Balder, Hoder, and other younger gods will return. Asgard will be rebuilt and a new All-Father, a creator god, will appear. Two humans will survive by hiding in the World Tree, and they will repopulate the world. [*See also* FATHER GOD; NORSE CREATION MYTHS; ODIN.]

Rama's Quest for Sita

RAMA was the son of a great king. His own noble deeds earned Rama the right to marry the half-goddess SITA. However, Rama was later banished to the jungle through the trickery of his father's youngest wife. Sita and Rama's brother, Laksmana, went with him.

Fierce magic warriors called Rakshas lived in the jungle. One day a horrible Raksha princess asked Rama to marry her. When he turned her down, the creature attacked Sita. During the struggle, Laksmana wounded the princess. A vengeful Raksha army attacked, but Rama defeated them. His magic weapon—the bow of VISNU—had golden arrows that never missed. Later, a Raksha disguised as a deer lured Sita into the jungle and kidnapped her.

Rama began a QUEST for Sita. He and Laksmana traveled to the kingdom of the monkeys in search of her. The monkeys had seen the golden chariot of Ravana, the Raksha king, fly overhead. In the jungle below, they had found jewelry which Rama recognized. Sita had left a trail for him to follow.

Helped by other jungle creatures, Rama, Laksmana, and the monkeys found and attacked the hated Rakshas. Rama killed Ravana with his magic arrows. The battle was won and Sita was rescued.

Unfortunately, Rama thought Sita had been unfaithful during her captivity. She threw herself into a fire, but the fire god refused to burn her, proving her innocence. The couple returned to Rama's kingdom, but later Rama doubted his wife again and left her by a river. She roamed the jungle, where she gave birth to Rama's two sons. During this time, she stayed with Valmiki, who was the author of the *Ramayana*.

Twelve years later, Sita returned to Rama with their sons, who recited the *Ramayana*. Mother Earth convinced Rama of Sita's faithfulness, and the couple was reunited. [*See also* HANUMAN.]

Ramayana (rä mä´ yä nä) ☙

A seven-book record of ancient INDIAN MYTHOLOGY, the *Ramayana* was written in an ancient language called Sanskrit by the poet Valmiki sometime between 200 B.C. and A.D. 200. The *Ramayana* tells the story of the hero RAMA and the half-goddess SITA.

Raven (rāv´ ən) ☙

The TRICKSTER spirit Raven is a popular figure in NATIVE NORTH AMERICAN MYTHOLOGY from the Pacific Northwest. Many tales were told about Raven, sometimes calling him by different names. Like many tricksters, Raven was greedy and often foolish. But he was also very helpful to human beings. Sometimes he took human form. [*See also* RAVEN, ADVENTURES OF.]

Rebirth and Resurrection

☙ Deities and humans return from death in myths told by many cultures.

Native Americans often carved mythological figures on knives and other objects. This knife handle shows the trickster Raven.

Sometimes the rebirth is a reincarnation into a different life. Resurrection sometimes means moving to a celestial, or heavenly, realm. According to NATIVE NORTH AMERICAN MYTHOLOGY and NATIVE CENTRAL AND SOUTH AMERICAN MYTHOLOGY, the world and its people have been re-created or reborn several times.

In many stories of rebirth and resurrection, a deity, hero, or heroine is reborn to life on earth. In most cases, the resurrection of a dead god becomes the symbol of renewal for the society. Some dead heroes and deities, including QUETZALCOATL and King Arthur, are expected to return in the future. All of these stories also imply the possibility of eternal life.

In agricultural myths, the annual resurrection of a deity such as OSIRIS of EGYPTIAN MYTHOLOGY and PERSEPHONE of GREEK MYTHOLOGY ensures a new growing season. The resurrected

Adventures of Raven (rā′ vən)

RAVEN felt sorry for the people, who originally lived in the dark and cold. The TRICKSTER knew that a Great Chief had the Sun, Moon, and stars hidden away. In some stories, Raven had himself born to the Great Chief's daughter. In others, the daughter invited Raven to live with them. In either case, Raven was such a demanding child that the chief allowed him to play with the bright objects just to keep him happy. One by one, Raven stole the stars, Moon, and Sun and put them in the sky.

Raven also stole fire from the Snowy Owl, who would not share it with anyone else. In one myth, Raven disguised himself as a deer, dipped his bushy tail in pitch, visited Owl, and danced around the fire. When his tail caught on fire, Raven dashed away and took the fire to the Indians.

When Raven's three brothers were drowned by an evil uncle, Raven found them and brought them back. But, like the Egyptian god OSIRIS, who also returned from the dead, the boys did not become fully alive and were unhappy in the land of the living. They showed no emotions and no longer laughed, played, or even ate. Raven finally returned them to the water.

Although ravens were considered bad omens in many European myths, Raven was a hero to Native Americans. In some traditions, he was the creator deity. [*See also* COYOTE.]

animal in a story about the Cherokee Bear Man also represents a new season and the possibility of immortality. In some stories, rebirth takes place even after the person or deity

Rig Veda Creation (rig´ vād´ ə)

The stories from INDIAN MYTHOLOGY collected in the *RIG VEDA* include several CREATION myths. One text describes the first being, Purusa, who had a thousand heads and a thousand feet. The SACRIFICE and DISMEMBERMENT of Purusa brought our world into being.

When Purusa was killed, the bottom quarter of his body became the universe and his feet became the earth. His arms were turned into warriors, who were the founders of the warrior caste. (A caste is a class of people in Hindu society). Purusa's thighs became the common people, and his mouth became the god INDRA. His eye became the Sun, and his mind became the Moon. Plants and animals were formed from his sacrifice, as well as sacred words, rituals, and the Vedas (books of myths) themselves.

In another Indian myth, creation was due to WORLD PARENTS. The male principle, the Heavens, had a daughter who was the Earth. The fire god, Agni, inspired passion in the Heavens and the Earth, who mated. They brought about the birth of words, rituals, and minor deities.

According to another story, the god BRAHMA emerged from the PRIMAL WATERS and turned the dreams of the god VISNU into physical reality. Other Indian myths focused on the idea of opposites, which were considered necessary for existence. In one story, there was only CHAOS in the beginning. However, both being and nonbeing existed—and both were essential for creation to take place. When being and nonbeing united, order was brought to chaos and the world came into being.

This early Roman mosaic is the head of Autumn. Rebirth follows in the spring.

has been cut into many pieces. For example, the Blackfoot Indian hero KUTOYIS is killed, cooked, eaten, and resurrected four times.

Individuals are not always reborn in their original form. In Greek and Roman myths, ADONIS, HYACINTHUS, and NARCISSUS are all reborn as flowers. In North American Indian myths, the deity is often resurrected in the form of food for the people, as in the story of CORN MOTHER. [*See also* ALCESTIS; ARTHUR, KING; ATTIS; BAAL MYTHS; DIONYSUS; DYING GOD; FARO; FERTILITY MYTHS; FLOOD; GHOST DANCE; HERCULES; HOPI EMERGENCE; INANNA AND THE UNDERWORLD; LABYRINTH; LEMMINKAINEN'S

DEATH AND RESURRECTION; MAYA; NAVAJO EMERGENCE; PERSEPHONE, HADES, AND DEMETER; ROMULUS AND REMUS; TAMMUZ; UNDERWORLD, DESCENT TO.]

Rhiannon (re an´ en) 🐎 In the CELTIC MYTHOLOGY collected in the *MABINOGION*, Rhiannon was a beautiful Welsh goddess associated with FERTILITY MYTHS. She rode a great, white, magic horse and was sometimes identified as a horse goddess.

The legendary characters Romulus and Remus played an important role in Roman history.

Romulus and Remus
(räm´ yə ləs) (rē´ məs)

According to ROMAN AND ETRUSCAN MYTHOLOGY, Romulus was the founder of Rome. He and his twin brother Remus were the sons of Rhea Silvia, the daughter of King Numitor of Alba Longa. Numitor's brother, Amulius, forced him from power and made Rhea Silvia a vestal—a servant to the Latin goddess Vesta.

Rhea Silvia became pregnant by Mars, the god of war (known as ARES in GREEK MYTHOLOGY). When Romulus and Remus were born, Numitor put their mother, Rhea Silvia, in prison and set the babies adrift on the Tiber River. They were rescued and nursed by a she-wolf, then adopted by a herdsman and his wife. Romulus and Remus grew up and returned to Alba Longa, where they slew Amulius and made Numitor king again.

The brothers decided to found their own CITY, but could not agree upon a site. Remus wanted to build the city upon Aventine Hill, while Romulus was equally insistent on Palatine Hill. The brothers quarreled and fought, and Romulus slew Remus. Thus Romulus came to build Rome at its present location on the Tiber River—and the city was named after him.

Romulus invited people from far and wide to populate Rome. At first, men were its only inhabitants. But Romulus invited the neighboring Sabine tribe for a festival, and he and his fellow Romans kidnapped all the Sabine women. A brief war ensued, but soon the Romans and Sabines learned to live in peace.

Romulus ruled Rome for 37 years. When he died, his father, Mars, carried his spirit off to heaven. There he became the god Quirinus, one of the most important Roman deities. [*See also* REBIRTH AND RESURRECTION.]

Rudra Destroys the World (rüd′ rə)

According to INDIAN MYTHOLOGY, the supreme Hindu deity, VISNU, will one day bring about an APOCALYPSE by taking the form of Rudra, a storm god. This will happen at the end of a time known as the Kali Age, when humankind has become extremely wicked.

Rudra will first dry up all the waters of the earth, including its oceans, lakes, rivers, and streams. Then Rudra will produce seven suns, which will set fire to all the universe. Living things everywhere will try to flee—but to no avail. They will all be consumed by the flames.

When nothing remains but cinders, Rudra will bring a tremendous downpour, producing a FLOOD that fills all the universe. Eventually, Visnu will discard the form of Rudra and begin CREATION anew. The story of Rudra destroying the world is told in the *RIG VEDA*.

According to the stories, King Pwyll spotted a beautiful lady as she rode by and tried to overtake her. Although he used his swiftest horses, and Rhiannon never seemed to change her slow pace, Pwyll could not catch up with her. When he at last called and asked her to wait for him, Rhiannon stopped, told the king her name, and announced that she had come to be his bride. A year later, Rhiannon and Pwyll were married. Rhiannon once made a trip to the Underworld to rescue their son,

Pyderi. [*See also* GREAT GODDESS; UNDERWORLD, DESCENT TO.]

Rig Veda (rig′ vād′ ə) ☙ The most ancient stories in INDIAN MYTHOLOGY were collected in four books called Vedas, written between 1500 and 500 B.C. (The word *veda* means "divine knowledge.") The *Rig Veda* is the oldest and most important of these four books. The Vedas contain hymns, prayers, rituals, sacred knowledge, and popular stories of gods and goddesses, heroes and heroines. They include several different CREATION myths, and also the story of a final APOCALYPSE. [*See also* BRAHMA; DANU; DURGA; INDRA; KALI; RIG VEDA CREATION; RUDRA DESTROYS THE WORLD; SIVA.]

Roman and Etruscan Mythology (rō′ mən) (i trəs′ kən) ☙ The myths of the Romans and Etruscans reflected their interest in order and stability. Though they resembled stories in GREEK MYTHOLOGY, they gave less attention to the personal lives of the gods. In some Roman myths, the deities corresponded to Greek deities. Other stories, such as those about ROMULUS AND REMUS, were specifically concerned with Rome. AENEAS, a character in the Greek epic poem, the *ILIAD*, went on to found Rome in a Roman work, the *AENEID*. The god APOLLO appeared in the PANTHEONS of both the Greeks and the Romans. [*See also* ADONIS; JUNO; JUPITER; PANDORA; SIBYL; VENUS.]

Sacrifice 🐦 The offering of the life of a plant, animal, or human to a deity is called a sacrifice. A HERO AND HEROINE might also sacrifice something of value for an important purpose. For example, the Norse god ODIN sacrificed one of his eyes to gain knowledge. In myths dealing with DISMEMBERMENT, a god or first human was sacrificed to create the world. In stories about a DYING GOD and other FERTILITY MYTHS, a deity was often sacrificed to be reborn every year. [*See also* DRAGONS; MANU; MAYAN CREATION MYTHS; PROMETHEUS; RIG VEDA CREATION; SIBYL; WANJIRU.]

Saturn 🐦 *See* CRONOS.

Sedna (sed´nə) 🐦 The Underworld goddess of Inuit myths, Sedna was first a young woman who refused to marry any man. In different versions of the story, she married a bird or a dog, which her father then killed. The father threw Sedna out of his boat and chopped off her fingers. Her fingers became the sea creatures, and they killed the father. [*See also* NATIVE NORTH AMERICAN MYTHOLOGY.]

Separation of Heaven and Earth 🐦 In many CREATION stories, an original CHAOS separated into heaven and earth. Sometimes this happened through the action of a deity and sometimes without any outside help. In some myths the separation of WORLD PARENTS—such as the Egyptian GEB AND NUT or Rangi and Papa in the myths of the Maori of New Zealand—represented the separation of heaven and earth.

In CHINESE CREATION MYTHS, the first being was a giant named PHAN KU, who grew larger every day. As his size increased, Phan Ku's head pushed the heavens away from the earth. A spiritual separation between gods and human beings was sometimes marked by the withdrawal of the deities from the earth to the heavens. [*See also* AFRICAN MYTHOLOGY; EARTH DIVER; EGYPTIAN CREATION MYTHS; FATHER GOD; GAIA; GREAT GODDESS; GREEK CREATION MYTHS; JAPANESE CREATION MYTHS; *LEABHAR GABHALA*; MAORI CREATION MYTHS; ZUNI CREATION MYTHS.]

Seth (seth´) 🐦 In EGYPTIAN MYTHOLOGY, Seth was the evil brother of the god-king OSIRIS. Because

This Egyptian painting shows Seth riding in a boat.

Seth was jealous and wanted the throne of Egypt for himself, he had Osiris killed. Seth was later killed by HORUS, the son of Osiris.

Shamans (shä´ mənz) 🐾 Cultures throughout the world honor healers, medicine men or women, and mystics; these figures are often called shamans. Shamans often have access to supernatural levels of knowledge and reality. In some cultures they are said to make use of the power of everything in nature, as well as to contact the spirits of dead ancestors. Shamans are sometimes important storytellers who pass along a culture's traditions. [*See also* ANCESTOR WORSHIP; ANIMISM; AUSTRALIAN ABORIGINAL MYTHOLOGY; FROG AND WIYOT; INCAN FLOOD; NATIVE NORTH AMERICAN MYTHOLOGY; WANJIRU.]

Sibyl (sib´ əl) 🐾 A sibyl was a woman who could predict the future by receiving inspiration from a deity. Sibyls appeared in GREEK MYTHOLOGY and ROMAN AND ETRUSCAN MYTHOLOGY. Early Christian stories name 12 sibyls, each identified with a prophecy.

The most fameous sibyl in Roman myths was the Sibyl of Cumae, who helped the hero AENEAS decend to and return from the Underworld.

The Sibyl of Cumae also offered the Roman king Tarquin a set of nine books that told the future of Rome. The Sibylline books were kept in a temple and consulted by the Romans in emergencies. A sibyl was also credited with writing the *Sibylline Oracles*, a collection of second- and third-century Judeo-Christian books of sayings and advice. [*See also* UNDERWORLD, DESCENT TO.]

Siegfried (sig´ frēd) 🐾 Stories of the hero Siegfried are among the most exciting in GERMANIC MYTHOLOGY. His magic cloak made him invisible. When he was a boy, Siegfried killed a DRAGON and smeared himself with its blood, mak-

Sita, the devoted wife of Rama, was considered a model of righteousness.

ing himself nearly invulnerable. The *NIBELUNGENLIED* tells about his relationship with BRYNHILD. In the Scandanavian epics, the EDDAS, Siegfried was called Sigurd. [*See also* HERO AND HEROINE; MONSTER SLAYING.]

Sita (sē´tä) 🔊 In the *RAMAYANA*, an important source of INDIAN MYTHOLOGY, the princess and half-goddess Sita represented the perfect Hindu wife. She followed her husband RAMA into exile, was captured by evil magic creatures called Rakshas, and was rescued by Rama. Her husband later abandoned her, but after many years they were reconciled. [*See also* HANUMAN.]

Siva (shē´və) 🔊 Siva (also known as Shiva) is one of the highest deities in INDIAN MYTHOLOGY. The god of nature, the arts, learning, dancing, revelry, and reproduction, Siva is both a destroyer and a creator. He is also the god of reintegration, a process by

which all the parts are brought together again to form a new whole.

According to Indian stories, Siva and his wife PARVATI made their home on the golden MOUNTAIN named Meru, which was considered the axis on which the world turned. He once bested the goddess KALI in a fierce, competitive dance. [*See also* BRAHMA; GANESA; GANGES, BIRTH OF THE; PANTHEONS; *RIG VEDA*; VISNU.]

The god Siva had a third eye in his forehead, which could destroy with a glance.

Sioux Creation Myths (sü´)

According to the NATIVE NORTH AMERICAN MYTHOLOGY of the Sioux Indians, Inyan was the first deity. His spirit was strong in the powerful and mysterious creative force called *Wakan Tanka*, which was possessed by everything in nature. Inyan let the blood flow out of his own veins, and the world was created from it. But Inyan was weakened by the loss of blood and lost his power.

Nevertheless, the creative power of his blood was now in the earth. The *Wakan Tanka* the earth was so great that some of it separated and formed another spirit, called Skan. The spirit of the earth was named Maka. The earth demanded light and warmth, so Skan created the sun. With each thing that was created, a new spirit also came into being. Soon Skan had to establish order among all the new deities as they struggled for power. He put a new spirit named Wi at the top, then himself, then Maka.

After everything quieted down, each spirit created a companion. Inyan created wisdom, or Ksa. Skan created the wind, Maka created passion, and Wi created the Moon. For a time, the new deities acted as servants to the original ones. But Ksa did not believe that arrangement was appropriate. He suggested creating a new pair of beings to be servants. So the deities took bits of themselves—bone, blood, wisdom, and beauty—and made two lesser creatures named Ate and Hun. These lesser creatures began to reproduce on their own, and their descendants populated the earth. [*See also* CREATION; DISMEMBERMENT.]

Sky Girl
In the NATIVE NORTH AMERICAN MYTHOLOGY of the Iroquois Indians, Sky Girl was the first woman. She lived in the heavens until one day she fell to earth through a hole in the clouds. At that time, the earth was covered with PRIMAL WATERS, but animals quickly spread out some mud and created an island for her to live on. In most versions of the Sky Girl story, she became either the mother or grandmother of twins—one who was good and one who was evil.

There are many Native American myths about a woman who fell from the sky. According to some stories, Sky Girl was thrown from the clouds by her jealous husband who suspected her of betrayal. In other versions she is a creator goddess, but she is also a destroyer responsible for fatal diseases. In some myths her name is Star Woman, and the Navajo Indians called her First Woman. [*See also* EARTH DIVER; EVE; LILITH; PANDORA; STAR WOMAN AND THE TWINS.]

Spider Woman
In the NATIVE NORTH AMERICAN MYTHOLOGY of the Southwest, Spider Woman was the Earth Goddess. She might be the single creator or work with another creator such as TAWA. She is sometimes called Spider Grandmother. According to a Cherokee myth, Spider Grandmother brought light to the people. She spun a web that reached to the other side of the world, traveled along it, and stole the sun from greedy

Star Woman and the Twins

NATIVE NORTH AMERICAN MYTHOLOGY includes CREATION stories about a woman called Star Woman who fell from the sky. According to the Seneca Indians, at first all people lived in the sky with the Great Chief. The earth was covered with water, and only waterbirds and creatures such as Turtle and Toad lived there.

When the Great Chief's daughter became ill, a wise man dreamed of a way to cure her. They put the girl next to a tree, uprooted it, and left her near the hole. But a man came along who was angry that the tree had been dug up. He kicked the girl into the hole, and she fell into empty space.

Birds saw Star Woman falling and caught her on their wings. By the time they reached the water, the birds were tired, so they put Star Woman on Turtle's back. Turtle eventually got tired, too. Then the birds asked Toad to dive into the water and bring back some mud. Toad put the mud onto Turtle's back. Both the mud and Turtle's back spread out, making the land.

Star Woman gave birth to a daughter, who helped her work the land. The daughter gave birth to twins named Flint and Sapling. Star Woman put Flint into a tree because she did not like him, but Sapling took a bow and arrows to his brother so he could get food. Finally Sapling brought Flint home. Together they made the earth bigger and created animals. The twins disagreed so much that they fought, and Sapling killed Flint. [See also EARTH DIVER; EVE; PANDORA; PRIMAL WATERS.]

Spider Woman is represented on this clay disk.

beings who had refused to share it. [See also ANANSE; CREATION; GREAT GODDESS; HOPI EMERGENCE.]

Star Woman 🐢 See STAR WOMAN AND THE TWINS.

Stone 🐢 In myths from various cultures, stones are said to have great power. They were often used as a place of SACRIFICE. Stones were also placed in holy sites, such as TEMPLES. Stone gods appeared in the mythology of many cultures. NATIVE NORTH

Sumerian/Babylonian Flood
(sü mer´ē ən) (bab ə lō´nē ən)

An early myth of a great FLOOD sent by deities to cleanse the earth was told in the Sumerian epic the *ENUMA ELISH*. The same story appeared in the Babylonian epic *GILGAMESH*. It is similar to the story of Noah in the Bible.

Enlil—the god of earth, air, and storms—became angry with human beings and decided to flood the earth. But the god of the waters, called ENKI or Ea, had created humans and wanted to save them. Enki warned one man, called Utnapishtim in the *Gilgamesh* story, that the flood was coming. He told Utnapishtim how to build a ship, or ark, large enough to save his family, and many other living things.

It rained for seven days and seven nights, but the ark survived the storm. It finally landed on Mount Nisir. Utnapishtim sent out a dove and a swallow, both of which came back. Then he sent out a raven. When it did not return, he knew there must be dry land nearby. So the people and creatures in the ark went to live on land again. [*See also* APOCALYPSE; APACHE CREATION MYTHS; FARO; INCAN FLOOD; MANABOZHO; MANU; MAYAN CREATION MYTHS; MOUNTAIN; NAVAJO EMERGENCE; PROMETHEUS; RUDRA DESTROYS THE WORLD.]

Sumerian Mythology (sü mer´ē ən) 🔊 The Sumerians developed the first high culture in Mesopotamia—a region in southeastern Iraq—about 3500 B.C. Although they were eventually absorbed into other groups, the Sumerians had a major influence on later civilizations of that area. Gilgamesh was a hero in Sumerian mythology before an epic was written about him by the ancient Babylonians. [*See also* ASSYRIAN MYTHOLOGY; BABYLONIAN MYTH-OLOGY; CITY; ENKI; *GILGAMESH*; INANNA-ISHTAR; SUMERIAN/BABYLONIAN FLOOD; TAMMUZ.]

The Sumerians developed a system of "picture" writing called cuneiform, which they used to record myths and to conduct business.

AMERICAN MYTHOLOGY, for example, includes Iroquois deities called Stone Giants. Stones also posed a challenge or test, such as when Arthur in CELTIC MYTHOLOGY became King after pulling a sword from a stone. [*See also* MOUNTAIN; TREE.]

T

Ta'aroa (tä ä rō´ ä) 🐚 In POLY-
NESIAN MYTHOLOGY, Ta'aroa was the
creator of the earth and sea and the
greatest god in the PANTHEON of
deities. In some legends, he hatched
from a cosmic egg and used its pieces
in the CREATION of the world. According to other stories, Ta'aroa created a
female and together they made the
sea, sky, and earth. He made the first
man from red earth, then took a bone
from the man's body and made the first
woman. When Ta'aroa became angry
with human beings, he caused the sea
to FLOOD the whole world, leaving only
the Polynesian islands above water.

Tammuz (tä´ müz) 🐚 A fertili-
ty god in SUMERIAN MYTHOLOGY,
Tammuz was the husband of Ishtar,
who mourned his death and rescued
him from the Underworld. Like the
Greek goddess PERSEPHONE, Tam-
muz spent part of every year in the
Underworld, and the rest of the year
among the living. [*See also* DYING GOD;
FATHER GOD; FERTILITY MYTHS; INANNA-
ISHTAR; REBIRTH AND RESURRECTION;
UNDERWORLD, DESCENT TO.]

Tawa (tä´ wä) 🐚 In the NATIVE
NORTH AMERICAN MYTHOLOGY of the
Hopi Indians, Tawa was supreme
deity of the Above. He and SPIDER
WOMAN created the earth. Tawa
formed pictures in his mind and Spider
Woman turned them into the physical
animals and people. After the CRE-
ATION, Tawa went to live in the sky as
the Sun God. [*See also* BRAHMA; FATHER
GOD; HOPI EMERGENCE; WORLD PARENTS.]

Temple 🐚 People of most cultures have built temples—places
to worship deities. Temples were

The Sumerian god Tammuz also
appeared in Babylonian mythology.

dedicated to many of the gods and goddesses. At their temples, the deities met with humans, answered questions, and gave blessings or curses. Priests and priestesses often resided in temples, sometimes serving as oracles. An oracle was a shrine where a priestess, inspired by a deity, made prophecies and gave advice. Many ancient temples were constructed to track changes in the seasons.

The sites of temples were considered sacred, and often one temple after another was built on the same spot. Some of the ancient buildings may have represented a sacred MOUNTAIN. [*See also* KUAN YIN; PAN-

THEONS; PERSEPHONE, HADES, AND DEMETER; SIBYL; STONE.]

Theogony (thē äg´ ə nē)

One of the most important sources of information about GREEK MYTHOLOGY, the *Theogony* relates the CREATION of the universe and the gods. The poem was written by Hesiod, who is believed to have been a farmer who lived in Greece around 800 B.C.

Theseus (thē´ sē əs)

A great hero in GREEK MYTHOLOGY, Theseus killed the Minotaur, a bull-like monster, who lived in the LABYRINTH, a maze built by King Minos of Crete. Theseus was said to be the son of either King Aegeus of Athens or the sea god POSEIDON. His mother was Aethra, the daughter of a king. [*See also* ARIADNE; THESEUS, ADVENTURES OF.]

Thor (thôr´)

In NORSE MYTHOLOGY, Thor was the large, red-bearded

This temple in India was dedicated to the god Siva.

The hero Theseus is shown here being reunited with his family after his return to Athens.

Adventures of Theseus (thē´ sē əs)

The Greek hero THESEUS is best known for his adventure on the island of Crete. His mother was Aethra, the daughter of King Pittheus. Under a spell cast by the witch MEDEA, Pittheus got Aegeus, the visiting king of Athens, drunk and sent him to bed with Aethra. According to some stories, the god POSEIDON also visited Aethra that night, leaving the paternity of Theseus in doubt. Before Aegeus returned to Athens, he told Aethra that if they had a son, the boy should be raised quietly for his protection. Aegeus put his sword and sandals under a heavy stone, and said that his son should bring them to Athens when he could do so. So Theseus grew up with his mother. When he was strong enough, he lifted the stone and took his father's sword and sandals.

On his way to Athens, Theseus fought and won many battles. His adventures made him famous all over the land, and he was welcomed in Athens as a great hero and the heir to his father's throne. At that time, Athens had to give Minos, the king of Crete, seven young men and seven young women every nine years as a sacrifice. Minos fed these young people to a monster called the Minotaur. When the time came for King Aegeus to send a new group to their deaths, Theseus volunteered to go.

After Theseus arrived in Crete, ARIADNE, the daughter of King Minos, fell in love with him. Theseus promised to marry Ariadne if she helped him survive the Minotaur. The half-human and half-bull monster lived in the LABYRINTH, a complicated maze. Ariadne gave Theseus a spool of thread to unroll behind him as he walked through the labyrinth, so that he could tell where he had been. Theseus found the Minotaur, killed it, and followed the thread back to freedom.

On the way back to Athens, Theseus abandoned Ariadne on an island. He also forgot that he had promised to put a white sail on his ship as a signal to his father that he was still alive. When King Aegeus saw a black sail on the approaching ship, he thought his son was dead. The king killed himself, and Theseus was declared king. Theseus had many more adventures, including a visit to the Amazons, a race of women warriors. [*See also* FATHER, SEARCH FOR; MONSTER SLAYING; MONSTERS AND MYTHICAL BEASTS.]

god of war. Lightning flashed when Thor struck his hammer, Mjollnir, against stone. When he threw the hammer, Thor caused thunderbolts, and the wheels of his chariot made the sound of thunder. Thor enjoyed eating, drinking, and fighting. A defender of Asgard, the home of the warrior gods known as the Aesir, he was the greatest enemy of the Giants, a race of supernatural beings. Thor's name was the origin of the word Thursday.

Destruction of Tiamat (tē´ ä mät)

In BABYLONIAN MYTHOLOGY the story of Tiamat is about both CREATION and destruction. According to the story, which was recorded in the *ENUMA ELISH*, the gods were frequently at war after the creation of the world. Tiamat's husband, Apsu, was killed by unruly younger gods named Lahmu and Lahamu. Tiamat then married the god Kingu, but she was still angry over the death of Apsu. In her fury, Tiamat created monsters that the young gods could not control. War broke out between the younger gods and Tiamat's monsters.

For a time, the younger gods were helpless against these terrible monsters. They turned to the storm god, MARDUK, for help and promised to make him the ruler of all creation if he defeated Tiamat.

Marduk bravely confronted the gigantic, dragonlike Tiamat face-to-face. First, he threw his net over her. Tiamat opened her mouth to swallow him whole; but Marduk blew a mighty wind into her mouth and shot an arrow inside it, splitting her heart.

Marduk maimed Tiamat's body horribly, using it to create the universe as we know it today. He cut her in two, making the upper half of her body the Heavens and the lower half the Earth. The other gods kept their promise to make Marduk their king, and he built his palace upon the Earth.

This story of Tiamat is similar to myths of later cultures, including the story of how ZEUS and the other Olympian gods defeated the Titans in GREEK CREATION MYTHS. [*See also* ASSYRIAN MYTHOLOGY; DISMEMBERMENT; DRAGONS; DYING GOD; GREAT GODDESS; MONSTER SLAYING; MONSTERS AND MYTHICAL BEASTS; SEPARATION OF HEAVEN AND EARTH.]

The god Thor enjoyed fighting, feasting, and drinking.

Tiamat (tē´ ä mät) 🐦 According to BABYLONIAN MYTHOLOGY, Tiamat was the dragonlike goddess of the salt sea. She represented CHAOS and PRIMAL WATERS. Tiamat's first husband was Apsu, the god of fresh waters. By mixing together, they gave birth to the gods Lahmu and Lahamu. Tiamat was eventually killed by the storm god MARDUK. [*See also* ASSYRIAN MYTHOLOGY; DRAGONS; DYING GOD; *ENUMA ELISH;* GREAT GODDESS; TIAMAT, DESTRUCTION OF.]

Tree 🐦 The mythologies of many cultures describe trees as powerful or sacred. Many stories describe a great World Tree that reaches from the center of the Earth to the Heavens and supports the world. In myths and religious traditions, trees are often associated with wisdom or knowledge. In the

Forests were powerful and mysterious places to ancient peoples, and trees often became associated with various good and bad spirits.

Tree that Holds Up the World

According to stories told by the Cheyenne Indians, a huge TREE holds up the world. Its trunk is somewhere in the north, but nobody knows exactly where. The tree supports the world and prevents it from falling into a bottomless void.

The tree that holds up the world has been there for a very long time. So has the Great White Grandfather Beaver who gnaws at it. Sometimes Grandfather Beaver chews slowly. But when he is annoyed he gnaws faster and faster. The Cheyenne believe that Grandfather Beaver has already gnawed halfway through the tree trunk. When he gets all the way through, the world will crash into the great nothingness. For that reason, the Cheyenne do not eat beaver or use their skins. They are very careful not to make Grandfather Beaver angry, so the world will last as long as possible. The myth of the tree that holds up the world is an APOCALYPSE story, predicting how the world will end. [*See also* NATIVE NORTH AMERICAN MYTHOLOGY.]

story of ADAM and EVE, they were forbidden to eat the fruit of the tree of knowledge. In Indian tradition, Buddha found enlightenment while sitting under the bodhi tree. And in NORSE MYTHOLOGY, the god ODIN hung himself on the tree Yggdrasil to gain wisdom.

Some trees are strongly connected with deities. In GREEK MYTHOLOGY, the olive tree was sacred to the goddess ATHENA. The Greek and Phrygian god ATTIS died on or beneath a pine tree, which was sacred to the goddess CYBELE.

People or NATURE SPIRITS became trees in some stories. For example, the nymph Daphne was turned into a laurel for her own protection when she was pursued by the god APOLLO. Tree nymphs also appear in INDIAN MYTHOLOGY. According to ancient NORSE MYTHOLOGY the first man and woman—Ash and Elm—were created from trees. [*See also* BALDER; COYOTE; FARO; FINNIC CREATION MYTHS; *GILGAMESH*; HAINUWELE; JAPANESE MYTHOLOGY; LONE MAN; MANABOZHO; OKANAGON MOTHER; ORPHEUS; OSIRIS; RAGNAROK, END

OF THE WORLD; TREE THAT HOLDS UP THE WORLD; WIYOT.]

Trials and Tests

In the myths of many lands, a hero or heroine faced a series of trials and tests to prove courage or accomplish an aim. Some, such as JASON, BEOWULF, and Gilgamesh, actively sought trials to demonstrate their valor. Others also faced trials voluntarily, but for different reasons. The Greek hero HERCULES undertook his labors as a penance for a misdeed. And according to INDIAN MYTHOLOGY, the half-goddess SITA threw herself into a fire to prove her innocence.

Sometimes trials and tests were imposed by others. In CELTIC MYTHOLOGY, physical tests were required of those who wanted to join the band of warriors called the Fianna. In GREEK MYTHOLOGY, the Sphinx—a monster that was part-human and part-animal—demanded that passersby answer a riddle. She devoured those who failed, until the tragic hero OEDIPUS destroyed her by answering correctly. The hero twins of the *POPUL VUH* and the Sumerian goddess INANNA confronted trials in the Underworld. [*See also* ARTHURIAN LEGEND; FINN AND THE FIANNA; GRAIL QUEST; HERO AND HEROINE; JOURNEY QUEST; MAYAN CREATION MYTHS; MONSTERS AND MYTHICAL BEASTS; MONSTER SLAYING; ODIN; QUEST; UNDERWORLD, DESCENT TO.]

Trickster (trik´ stər)

Foolish and wise at the same time, the trickster is one of the most popular characters in mythology. Tricksters are especially popular in NATIVE NORTH AMERICAN MYTHOLOGY and AFRICAN MYTHOLOGY. Tricksters can be human beings, animals, or something in between. They are usually male, although some are female.

Tricksters are clowns, practical jokers, and often cheats. Sometimes their jokes backfire and they are tricked by others. In some stories, tricksters are the creators of the world and helpers to humankind. They also provide land for people to live on, bring them fire, or teach them agriculture and important crafts. [*See also* ANANSE; CARIBBEAN MYTHOLOGY; COYOTE; DIKITHI; EARTH DIVER; EDDAS; GLOOSCAP; HERMES; HERO AND HEROINE; INKTOMI; KRISHNA; LEGBA; LOKI; MANABOZHO; MARDUK; MAUI; MAWU; MONSTER SLAYING; NATIVE CENTRAL AND SOUTH AMERICAN MYTHOLOGY; NAVAJO EMERGENCE; OLD MAN; RAVEN.]

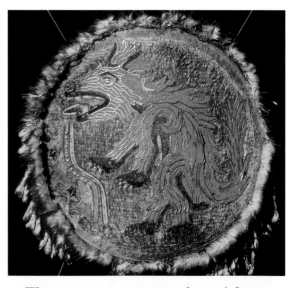

The coyote was a popular trickster figure in Native North American mythology.

U V W

Underworld, Descent to

In the myths of many cultures, a hero and/or heroine journeys to the Underworld, which is usually the land of the dead. The purpose of the journey may be to visit, question, or bring back someone who has died and resides there. Sometimes the hero is being tested. In stories based on the "ORPHEUS" THEME, a hero brings a loved one back from the Underworld, only to lose her again because he disobeys a command not to look back at her or touch her. In many myths, a DYING GOD figure goes to the Underworld each fall and is reborn each spring, bringing about the change of seasons for a new agricultural cycle.

Traveling to the Underworld could be difficult. In NORSE MYTHOLOGY, the eight-legged horse of the god ODIN could carry a rider there, and the goddess FREYA flew there with her falcon-skin cloak. On a trip to see his dead father, the Roman hero AENEAS was guided past many dangers by the SIBYL of Cumae.

The mythical Underworld is not always the land of the dead. In the EMERGENCE stories of NATIVE NORTH AMERICAN MYTHOLOGY, humans, animals, and supernatural beings lived within the earth before they migrated to the surface. And in CELTIC MYTHOLOGY the Underworld god Midir ruled over a magical fairyland. [*See also* ACHILLES; AFTERLIFE; ALCESTIS; APACHE CREATION MYTHS; APHRODITE AND ADONIS; BAAL MYTHS; BALDER; *BOOK OF THE DEAD*; CUPID AND PSYCHE; DIONYSUS; ENKI; HADES; HAINUWELE; HECATE; HERCULES; HERO AND HEROINE; INANNA-ISHTAR; JAPANESE CREATION MYTHS; JOURNEY QUEST; KUAN YIN; MIDIR AND ETAIN; MWINDO; ODYSSEUS; ORPHEUS AND EURYDICE; PERSEPHONE, HADES, AND DEMETER; QUEST; RA; REBIRTH AND RESURRECTION; RHIANNON; SEDNA; TAMMUZ; TRIALS AND TESTS; WANJIRU.]

Uranus (yùr´ ən əs)

The earliest god of the heavens in GREEK MYTHOLOGY, Uranus was created by the Mother Goddess GAIA. Together they produced the Titans, the first PANTHEON of Greek gods. Uranus was castrated by his son CRONOS, who became the father of ZEUS and the Olympian gods. [*See also* GREAT GODDESS.]

Vainamoinen (vi nə moi´nen)

The first man according to FINNIC MYTHOLOGY, Vainamoinen cleared the land and planted seeds. His mother was the Air Spirit and his father was the Sea. He knew how to use the symbolic writing called runes, and he had magic powers. A gifted singer and musician, Vainamoinen was a wise old man, apparently from birth. He was once pledged to marry a woman named Aino, but she rejected him because he seemed so old. [*See also* FINNIC CREATION MYTHS; *KALEVALA;* LEMMINKAINEN'S DEATH AND RESURRECTION.]

Venus (vē´ nəs) ☙ *See* APHRODITE.

Visnu (vēsh´ nü) ☙ One of the three great gods in INDIAN MYTHOLOGY, Visnu is the deity of goodness and

The god Visnu was a popular subject in ancient Indian art. This work dates from the 1100s.

mercy and the protector of the world. He has had many avatars (forms of himself on earth), including RAMA and KRISHNA, all of whom came to our world to help human beings. The Ganges River in India is said to flow from the toe of Visnu, and according to some Indian creation myths, the world was first dreamed by Visnu, then made physical by the god BRAHMA. [*See also* GANGES, BIRTH OF THE; *MAHABHARATA; RAMAYANA; RIG VEDA;* SIVA.]

Wanjiru (wän jē´ rü) ☙ In AFRICAN MYTHOLOGY, once when there was a terrible three-year drought a young woman named Wanjiru agreed to be sacrificed as part of a rainmaking ceremony. Her parents agreed to sell her, and during the ceremony Wanjiru was swallowed up by the earth. She was brought back from the Underworld by a warrior who loved her. [*See also* SACRIFICE; UNDERWORLD, DESCENT TO.]

Waterjar Boy ☙ In the NATIVE NORTH AMERICAN MYTHOLOGY of the Tewa Indians, Waterjar Boy was born in the form of a clay pot. When he reached adolescence, he broke the pot and emerged as a handsome boy. In his human form, he proved to be a great hunter. His story includes a miraculous birth and a JOURNEY QUEST in search of his father. [*See also* WATERJAR BOY, ADVENTURES OF; FATHER, SEARCH FOR.]

White Buffalo Woman ☙ In the NATIVE NORTH AMERICAN MYTH-

OLOGY of the Sioux Indians, White Buffalo Woman was a deity who taught the people many important skills. She emphasized respect for the earth and responsibility to the tribe. As she departed from the Sioux, she took the forms of three different buffalo—including a white buffalo calf, the most sacred of all animals. According to legend, White Buffalo Woman will someday return to the Sioux. [*See also* ARTHUR, KING; QUETZALCOATL; WHITE BUFFALO WOMAN AND THE SIOUX.]

Wiyot (wē´ yät) 🐘 In the NATIVE NORTH AMERICAN MYTHOLOGY of the Shoshone Indians and some neighboring tribes, Wiyot was the deity who created human beings and animals. According to the story of FROG AND WIYOT, when Wiyot died his people burned his body, and a great oak tree grew up from his ashes. Wiyot then became the moon, and at night he looked down and continued to watch over his people. [*See also* FROG AND WIYOT.]

World Parents 🐘 In many myths from around the world, CREATION was the act of a couple. Often, the Heavens was the first father and Earth was the first mother. In EGYPTIAN CREATION MYTHS, however, the Heavens was the female Nut while the Earth was her male sibling Geb. In still other cultures, the female parent was represented as the PRIMAL WATERS.

Adventures of Waterjar Boy

The myth of WATERJAR BOY is about a young hero who finds his true identity. The story has been told by the Tewa Indians of New Mexico.

According to the story, a young woman stepped on a piece of clay while making pottery one day. The clay contained a seed that made her pregnant, even though she had never been alone with a man. When her child was born, he looked like a clay water jar instead of a human child. Waterjar Boy had no arms and legs, but he could roll along and play with the other boys and girls in the village. He talked and ate through the mouth of the jar.

One day Waterjar Boy went hunting with his grandfather. While chasing a rabbit, Waterjar Boy rolled down a hill and smashed against a tree. The clay pot shattered, but a handsome young man sprang out of the broken pieces. He went to find his grandfather, who at first did not believe that this was his grandson. Finally the old man was convinced, and the two went home.

Having overcome the difficulties of his birth, Waterjar Boy decided to find his father. He traveled to a spring where he met an old man named Red Water Snake. Waterjar Boy knew in his heart that Red Water Snake was his father, and he soon convinced the old man as well. Red Water Snake was glad to meet his son and introduced the boy to other relatives who lived in the spring. Sometime later Waterjar Boy's mother died, and the boy went to live in the spring. Red Water Snake brought the boy's mother to life, so they were all together. [*See also* FATHER, SEARCH FOR; HERO AND HEROINE; NATIVE NORTH AMERICAN MYTHOLOGY; QUEST.]

White Buffalo Woman and the Sioux (sü´)

The spirit called WHITE BUFFALO WOMAN taught the Sioux about the unity of life and respect for the earth. At one time the Sioux were having difficulty finding enough food, so the chief sent out two warriors to hunt. As the young men walked along, they saw a strange white figure approaching them. When the figure got nearer, the warriors could see that it was a beautiful woman. One of the men tried to grab her, but he was instantly burned to a pile of ashes and bones. The second warrior showed her the respect she deserved. She told him that she was White Buffalo Woman and that she had many important things to tell the Sioux people.

White Buffalo Woman returned to the village with the warrior. She gathered the people and took them to the medicine lodge. She showed them how to build an altar out of red earth in the center of the lodge. She drew a large circle on the ground and described the ring of life—the ways in which all things are connected. She said that the people would be destroyed, as the first warrior had been, if they did not show respect for the earth.

White Buffalo Woman also taught the people how to carry out religious rituals and how to use the sacred pipe. She described the four directions, the four ages of creation, and the proper roles for men, women, and children. She told the women and children that their roles were as sacred as those of the men. After White Buffalo Woman left, herds of buffalo came to the people and waited to be killed for food. [*See also* GREAT GODDESS.]

World parents were not necessarily gods, nor did they always show human traits. Rather, they often represented male and female principles in life. [*See also* ADAM; CHAOS; EVE; FATHER GOD; FERTILITY MYTHS; GEB AND NUT; GREAT GODDESS.]

Wulbari ✎ (wŭl bär´ ē) In the AFRICAN MYTHOLOGY of the Ashanti of Ghana, Wulbari is the high god who contends with the TRICKSTER character ANANSE. In the CREATION myth of the Tongo people, Wulbari is the sky god and is sometimes called Wularbi.

According to that story, at the beginning of time the sky was right on top of the earth. Human beings lived in a narrow space between the sky and the earth. However, the smoking fires that people made burned Wulbari's eyes. People also had a habit of wiping their hands on the sky when they were cleaning up after work. And it was even said that one woman sometimes cut off pieces of Wulbari to flavor her soup. That is why the god eventually moved much farther away from earth, to where the sky is now. [*See also* MAWU; SEPARATION OF HEAVEN AND EARTH.]

X Y Z

Ymir (ē´ mir) ✍ In NORSE CRE-
ATION MYTHS, Ymir was one of the
earliest beings. A frost giant, Ymir
and his family were formed by melting ice. In a typical DISMEMBERMENT
story about CREATION, the Norse god
ODIN and his two brothers killed Ymir
and made the world from the parts of
his body. They made Midgard, the
earth where humans would live, from
Ymir's eyebrows.

Zeus (züs) ✍ According to
GREEK MYTHOLOGY, Zeus was the
king of the gods of Mount Olympus.
He was the FATHER GOD who reigned
over the sky and all creation.

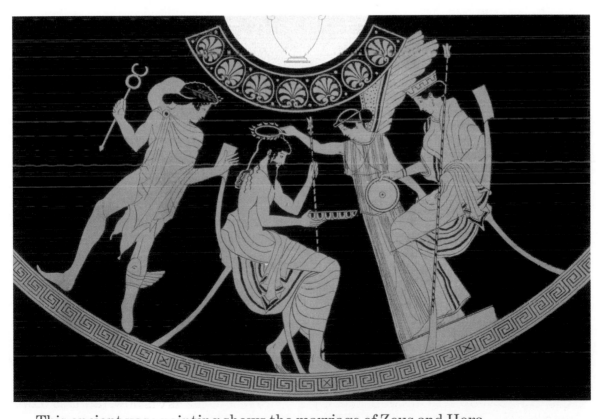

This ancient vase painting shows the marriage of Zeus and Hera.

Zuni Creation Myths (zü´ nē)

According to the myths of the Zuni Indians, CREATION began with only one being named Awonawilona. Alone in a great, dark, otherwise empty space, Awonawilona sent his thoughts into space. His thoughts created mists that could grow into other things. Awonawilona turned himself into the Sun god. The mist thickened and fell, becoming the sea. The power of the Sun brought life into the waters, creating Mother Earth and Father Sky.

This first couple created life on earth. Then Earth separated from Sky and sank into the water. Mother Earth was carrying children, but she did not want to give birth to them because she was worried about how they would know where they were and where they should live. To discuss the problem, Mother Earth and Father Sky took the form of a man and a woman.

The pair decided to create mountains to separate one region from another. Mother Earth made warm places for the people to live. Father Sky scattered glowing golden grains of corn in the heavens to guide the people when the Sun was not nearby. They made many other preparations for their children.

Soon the seeds of people and animals were growing in four caves in the earth. At first, the new beings crawled over each other, struggling, grumbling, and spitting. The most intelligent one, Poshaiyankya, came out of the cave alone. He begged the Sun to help the other creatures crawling in the darkness. The Sun and Mother Earth decided to start over.

This time Mother Earth gave birth to twins, called the Beloved Twain. These two, who had supernatural powers, were the ancestors of human beings. They went to the dark caves, got to know the lower creatures, and finally led them out into the light. [*See also* EMERGENCE; FATHER GOD; GREAT GODDESS; NATIVE NORTH AMERICAN MYTHOLOGY; SEPARATION OF HEAVEN AND EARTH.]

Part of Zeus' power came from his control of the thunderbolt. But as powerful as he was, he often found it difficult to keep his fellow gods under control. They frequently quarreled among themselves and even plotted against Zeus himself.

Zeus was often portrayed as wise, but just as often as foolish. He was frequently unfaithful to his wife, HERA— sometimes with mortal women. Among his many children by mortals were DIONYSUS, HELEN, and HERCULES. In Roman mythology, Zeus was known as Jupiter. [*See also* APHRODITE; APOLLO; ARES; ATHENA; CALYPSO; DEMETER; GREEK CREATION MYTHS; HADES; HEPHAESTUS; HERMES; JUPITER; LEDA AND THE SWAN; NARCISSUS; ODYSSEUS; ORPHEUS AND EURYDICE; PANDORA'S BOX; PERSEPHONE; PERSEUS; POSEIDON; PROMETHEUS; TIAMAT; URANUS.]

Selected Bibliography

African

Abrahams, Roger, ed. *African Folktales: Traditional Stories of the Black World.* New York: Pantheon Books, 1983.

Bennett, Martin. *West African Trickster Tales.* New York: Oxford University Press, 1994.

Pelton, Robert D. *The Trickster in West Africa: A Study of Mythic Irony and Sacred Delight.* Los Angeles: University of California Press, 1980.

Radin, Paul, Elinore Marvel, and James Johnson Sweeney, eds. *African Folktales & Sculpture.* New York: Bollingen Foundation/Pantheon Books, 1952.

Australian

Eliade, Mircea. *Australian Religions: An Introduction.* Ithaca: Cornell University Press, 1973.

Caribbean

Jackson, Guida M. *Encyclopedia of Traditional Epics.* Santa Barbara, Calif.: ABC-Clio, 1994.

Celtic and Anglo-Saxon

Bulfinch, Thomas. *The Age of Chivalry.* New York: New American Library, 1962.

Cavendish, Richard. *King Arthur and the Grail: The Arthurian Legends and Their Meaning.* London: Paladin, 1985.

Coleman, Wim, and Pat Perrin. *Retold Northern European Myths.* Logan, Iowa: Perfection Learning, 1994.

Gantz, Jeffrey. *Early Irish Myths and Sagas.* Harmondsworth, Middlesex: Penguin, 1981.

Green, Miranda Jane. *Dictionary of Celtic Myth and Legend.* London: Thames and Hudson, 1992.

Lacy, Norris J., ed. *The Arthurian Encyclopedia.* New York: Garland, 1986.

Rees, Alwyn, and Brinley Rees. *Celtic Heritage: Ancient Tradition in Ireland and Wales.* New York: Grove Press, 1961.

Squire, Charles. *Celtic Myth & Legend: Poetry and Romance.* New York: Bell Publishing, 1979.

Central and South American

Coe, Michael. *The Maya.* 5th ed. London: Thames and Hudson, 1993.

Nicholson, Irene. *Mexican and Central American Mythology.* Northants, England: Newnes Books, 1983.

Tedlock, Dennis, trans. *Popol Vuh: The Mayan Book of the Dawn of Life.* New York: Touchstone, 1985.

Chinese and Japanese

Aston, W. G., trans. *Nihongi: Chronicles of Japan from the Earliest Times to A.D. 697.* London: George Allen and Unwin, 1956.

Bonnefoy, Yves. *Asian Mythologies.* Translated by Wendy Doniger. Chicago: University of Chicago Press, 1993.

Philippi, Donald L., trans. *Kojiki.* Princeton, N.J.: Princeton University Press, 1969.

Piggot, Juliet. *Japanese Mythology.* New York: Paul Hamlyn, 1969.

Whittaker, Cleo, ed. *An Introduction to Oriental Mythology.* London: Grange Books, 1989.

Egyptian

Campbell, Joseph. *Primitive Mythology.* Vol. 1 of *The Masks of God.* New York: Penguin Books, 1959.

Rundle-Clark, R. T. *Myths and Symbols in Ancient Egypt.* London: Thames and Hudson, 1978.

Watterson, Barbara. *The Gods of Ancient Egypt.* New York: Facts on File, 1984.

Greek and Roman

Apollonius of Rhodes. *The Voyage of Argo.* Translated with an introduction by E. V. Rieu. London: Penguin Books, 1986.

Bulfinch, Thomas. *The Age of Fable.* New York: Airmont, 1965.

Coleman, William S. E., Jr., and Rebecca Spears Schwartz. *Retold Classic Myths.* Vol. 1. Logan, Iowa: Perfection Learning, 1990.

Coleman, William S. E., Jr., and Rebecca Spears Schwartz. *Retold Classic Myths.* Vol. 2. Logan, Iowa: Perfection Learning, 1990.

Graves, Robert. *The Greek Myths.* 2 vols. New York: Penguin Books, 1957.

Grimal, Pierre, et. al. *The Penguin Dictionary of Classical Mythology.* New York: Penguin Books, 1991.

Hamilton, Edith. *Mythology: Timeless Tales of Gods and Heroes.* New York: Mentor, 1969.

Hesiod. *The Works and Days, Theogony, and the Shields of Herakles.* Translated by Richard Lattimore. Ann Arbor: University of Michigan Press, 1973.

Homer. *The Odyssey*. Translated by Robert Fagles. New York: Penguin Books, 1996.

McCaughrean, Geraldine. *Greek Myths*. New York: Macmillan, 1993.

Price, Michele, and William S. E. Coleman, Jr. *Retold Classic Myths*. Vol. 1. Logan, Iowa: Perfection Learning, 1990.

Spretnak, Charlene. *Lost Goddesses of Early Greece: A Collection of Pre-Hellenic Myths*. 4th ed. Boston: Beacon Press, 1992.

Virgil. *The Aeneid*. Translated by Robert Fitzgerald. New York: Random House, 1983.

Hebrew

Ginzberg, Louis. *The Legends of the Jews*. 7 vols. Translated by Henrietta Szold. Philadelphia: Jewish Publication Society of America, 1909–1938.

Rappoport, Angelo S. *Myth and Legend of Ancient Israel*. 3 vols. London: Gresham, 1928.

Indian

Blackburn, Stuart. *Oral Epics in India*. Berkeley: University of California Press, 1989.

Bonnefoy, Yves. *Asian Mythologies*. Translated by Wendy Doniger. Chicago: University of Chicago Press, 1993.

O'Flaherty, Wendy D., trans. *Hindu Myths*. New York: VikingPenguin, 1975.

Whittaker, Cleo, ed. *An Introduction to Oriental Mythology*. London: Grange Books, 1989.

Middle Eastern

Hook, S. H. *Middle Eastern Mythology*. Middlesex, England: Penguin Books, 1963.

Kramer, Samuel Noah. *Sumerian Mythology*. New York: Harper & Row, 1961.

Kramer, Samuel Noah, et al. *Mythologies of the Ancient World*. New York: Doubleday, 1961.

Sandars, N. K. *The Epic of Gilgamesh: An English Version with an Introduction*. London: Penguin Books, 1972.

Multicultural

Bonnefoy, Yves. *Mythologies*. Vol. 1. Chicago: The University of Chicago Press, 1991.

Campbell, Joseph. *The Hero with a Thousand Faces*. Princeton, N. J.: Princeton University Press, 1973.

Coleman, Wim, and Pat Perrin. *Retold World Myths*. Logan, Iowa: Perfection Learning, 1993.

Cotterell, Arthur. *A Dictionary of World Mythology*. New York: Oxford University Press, 1986.

Evans, Ivor H., ed. *Brewer's Dictionary of Phrase & Fable*. 14th ed. New York: Harper & Row, 1989.

Gaster, Theodor. *The Oldest Stories in the World*. New York: Viking, 1956.

Hyde, Lewis. *Trickster Makes This World: Mischief, Myth, and Art*. New York: Farrar, Straus and Giroux, 1998.

Jackson, Guida M. *Encyclopedia of Traditional Epics*. New York: Oxford University Press, 1995.

Jordan, Michael. *Encyclopedia of Gods: Over 2,500 Deities of the World*. New York: Facts on File, 1993.

Kramer, Samuel Noah. *Mythologies of the Ancient World*. New York: Doubleday, 1961.

Leach, Maria, ed. *Funk & Wagnalls Standard Dictionary of Folklore, Mythology, and Legend*. San Francisco: Harper & Row, 1984.

Leeming, David. *Mythology. Pictorial narrative by Edwin Bayrd*. New York: Newsweek Books, 1976.

———. *Mythology: The Voyage of the Hero*. New York: Oxford University Press, 1998.

———. *The World of Myth: An Anthology*. New York: Oxford University Press, 1990.

Leeming, David Adams, ed. *Storytelling Encyclopedia: Historical, Cultural, and Multiethnic Approaches to Oral Traditions Around the World*. Phoenix: Oryx Press, 1997.

Leeming, David, with Margaret Leeming. *A Dictionary of Creation Myths*. New York: Oxford University Press, 1994.

Leeming, David, and Jake Page. *Goddess: Myths of the Female Divine*. New York: Oxford University Press, 1990.

New Larousse Encyclopedia of Mythology. Introduction by Robert Graves. New York: Paul Hamlyn, 1968.

Rosenberg, Donna. *World Mythology*. Lincolnwood, Ill.: Natonal Textbook Company, 1987.

Smith, Jonathan Z., ed. *The HarperCollins Dictionary of Religion*. New York: HarperCollins, 1995.

Sproul, Barbara C. *Primal Myths: Creating the World*. New York: Harper & Row, 1979.

Willis, Roy, ed. *World Mythology*. New York: Henry Holt, 1993.

Native American

Aoki, Haruo. *Nez Perce Narratives*. Berkeley: University of California Press, 1989.

Ayre, Robert. *Sketco the Raven*. Toronto: Macmillan, 1961.

Bright, William. *A Coyote Reader.* Berkeley: University of California Press, 1993.

Erdoes, Richard, and Alfonso Ortiz. *American Indian Myths and Legends.* New York: Pantheon Books, 1985.

Gill, Sam D., and Irene F. Sullivan. *A Dictionary of Native American Mythology.* New York: Oxford University Press, 1992.

Hynes, William J., and William G. Doty, eds. *Mythical Trickster Figures.* Tuscaloosa, Ala.: The University of Alabama Press, 1993.

Leeming, David, and Jake Page. *The Mythology of Native North America.* Norman, Okla.: University of Oklahoma Press, 1998.

Thompson, Stith. *Tales of the North American Indians.* Bloomington, Ind.: University Press, 1929.

Norse and Germanic

Branston, Brian. *Gods of the North.* New York: Thames and Hudson, 1980.

Coleman, Wim, and Pat Perrin. *Retold Northern European Myths.* Logan, Iowa: Perfection Learning, 1994.

Crossley-Holland, Kevin. *The Norse Myths.* Harmondsworth, Middlesex: Penguin Books, 1982.

Davidson, H. R. Ellis. *Gods and Myths of Northern Europe.* Harmondsworth, Middlesex: Penguin, 1964.

Evans, Cheryl, and Anne Millard. *Norse Myths and Legends.* Tulsa, Okla.: EDC Publishing, 1986.

Mackenzie, Donald A. *Teutonic Myth and Legend.* New York: William H. Wise, 1934.

Sturluson, Storri. *The Poetic Edda.* Translated by Henry Adams Bellows. Lewiston, N.Y.: E. Mellen Press, 1991.

Sturluson, Storri. *The Prose Edda.* Translated by Arthur Gilchrist Brodeur. New York: The American-Scandinavian Foundation, 1960.

Polynesian

Andersen, Johannes. *Myths and Legends of the Polynesians.* Rutland, Vt. and Tokyo, Japan: Charles E. Tuttle Co., 1969.

Pronunciation Guide

The mark ´ is placed after a syllable with a primary accent.

a	hat, cap	m	me, am	u	cup, butter		
ā	age, face	n	no, in	ù	full, put		
â	care, fair	ng	long, bring	ü	rule, move		
ä	father, far						
b	bad, rob	o	hot, rock	v	very, save		
ch	child, much	ō	open, go	w	will, woman		
d	did, red	o	all, caught	y	young, yet		
o	lot, boat	ô	order	z	zero, breeze		
ē	equal, be	oi	oil, voice	zh	measure, seizure		
èr	term, learn	ou	house, out				
f	fat, if	p	paper, cut	ə	represents:		
g	go, bag	r	run, try		a in about		
h	he, how	s	say, yes		e in taken		
i	it, pin	sh	she, rush		i in pencil		
ï	ice, five	t	tell, it		o in lemon		
		th	thin, both		u in circus		
j	jam, enjoy	ŦH	then, smooth				
k	kind, seek						
l	land, coal						

Source: *Thorndike-Barnhart Student Dictionary*

Index

Page numbers for main entries (including feature box titles) are in boldface. Page numbers for illustrations are in italics.